I Can Fix This

life

ALSO BY KRISTINA KUZMIČ

Hold On, But Don't Hold Still

I Can Fix This

*And Other Lies I Told
Myself While Parenting
My Struggling Child*

Kristina Kuzmič

PENGUIN LIFE

VIKING
An imprint of Penguin Random House LLC
penguinrandomhouse.com

A Penguin Life Book

LIBRARY OF CONGRESS CATALOGING-IN-PUBLICATION DATA
Names: Kuzmič, Kristina, author.
Title: I can fix this: and other lies I told myself while parenting
my struggling child / Kristina Kuzmič.
Description: [New York] : Penguin Life, [2024] |
Identifiers: LCCN 2024003456 (print) | LCCN 2024003457 (ebook) |
ISBN 9780593653333 (hardcover) | ISBN 9780593653340 (ebook)
Subjects: LCSH: Mothers and sons. | Child rearing. | Parenting. | Parents
of problem children. | Problem children. | Teenagers—Mental health.
Classification: LCC HQ755.85 .K89 2024 (print) | LCC HQ755.85 (ebook) |
DDC 306.874/3—dc23/eng/20240223
LC record available at https://lccn.loc.gov/2024003456
LC ebook record available at https://lccn.loc.gov/2024003457

Printed in the United States of America
1st Printing

Set in Bell MT Pro
Designed by Cassandra Garruzzo Mueller

Some names and identifying characteristics have been
changed to protect the privacy of the individuals involved.

For Jacy

Tell the story of the mountain you climbed.
Your words could become a page in someone
else's survival guide.

MORGAN HARPER NICHOLS

Author's Note

I am deeply touched that my book has found a spot on your reading list. Writing this—revisiting and trying to put into words the complex journey my family navigated—was cathartic, but also really painful at times. In our story, I candidly address suicidal ideation, substance abuse, self-harm, and other sensitive themes. If these topics stir up your own memories and vulnerabilities, I encourage you to be gentle with yourself and read with care. If you or someone you love are in the midst of tough and painful days, I urge you to reach out for all of the support you can. All my love to you and your family.

CONTENTS

Foreword

If I had a dollar for every parent I have coached in my office who exclaimed, *"I wish my child came with a map!"* I would be unimaginably wealthy. Sadly for us, our children don't come with any such instruction manual. We are thrown into parenthood's stormy waters without an oar or a life jacket, leaving many of us lost at sea. We pretend we know what we are doing but this pretense leads us into murkier quicksands of doubt and anxiety. But when we surrender to the vast complexities and unknowns of this journey, we can begin to seek and accept the help we so desperately need to survive the inevitable overwhelm and anguish of the journey. In short: parenting is one of the toughest jobs in the world, and every parent needs help.

Bearing witness to Kristina and her family's journey is like riding the rapids alongside them, and it will help you navigate your own parenting tidal waves. By offering us an in-depth account of her most vulnerable and maddening moments as a mother of a child in anguish, she offers us a story as close to an emotional road map as possible, so that the next time we are in our own parenting hell our steps will be illuminated by recollections of her wisdom and courage.

Every parent knows this truth: *there's nothing harder than raising a child.* And we all know that it's not just hard; it is often downright torturous—even traumatic. We know this truth but we pretend to the external world that parenthood is a walk in the park. The reason for this? We are ashamed to admit the brutal hardship of this journey. And why are we ashamed? Because our culture tells us that parenting "should be as natural as breathing." So if we experience pain, hardship, confusion, or failure, the problem must be us. So obsessed are we with raising these otherworldly beings that we lose sight of any sense of normalcy, humanity, and, dare I say, gratitude for the ordinary. What we don't realize is that this overzealous focus on excellence only leads us to feel great shame and unworthiness when our children (or ourselves) show any signs of weakness or frailty. This rigid expectation gets projected back onto our children, who then internalize a sense of self-loathing that spins into more inner disease. And the cycle of low self-worth perpetuates itself through generations.

Our identity as parents feels all-consuming, especially when we place all of our worth on this role. So when our children struggle and this role collapses on us, we feel as if we have failed to the greatest degree. If we aren't good at this, then what are we good at? Our entire sense of self, significance, and worth come into doubt. If our children experience failure and act in forbidden ways, then doesn't this mean we have failed them and society? How can we show our face to the world? Who will understand our plight? The separation between who our children are and who we are as mothers especially narrows to the point of oblivion. This fusion and enmeshment creates further confusion and overwhelm for all involved. We and our children can drown in this relational entanglement, each of us desperately gasping for air.

The fact is this: we all enter the parenting journey with great fantasies and expectations. We imagine picnics in the park, adventures at Disney World, and cozy bedtime rituals. We thought we would raise children who are cut from the cloth of great success, unparalleled achievement, and unrelenting happiness. So we work really hard from the start to help them shine brightly. We research the best options and enroll them in one activity after another. We push them to excel. No price is too high if it means our children's future success. This is just the way we are conditioned to parent.

But this outlook doesn't factor in any other reality. The possibility that our children might be bullied, or be socially awkward, have learning difficulties, be anxious or depressed, turn to addictions, or want to commit suicide is the furthest thing from our mind. So when these unavoidable complexities emerge in our lives, we feel thoroughly blindsided. Because no one shares how ubiquitous, how unavoidable, these realities are, we end up believing that setback, pain, hardship, and peril happen only *to* us and *because* of us. We are therefore consumed by tremendous loneliness, guilt, and shame. And so then we hide our reality from others even more. This is the greatest cover-up operation of all time. More and more parents disappear in the isolation created by this grand charade of perfectionism.

One of the main reasons I pioneered conscious parenting is to move us parents away from the delusion that we are supposed to be perfect and raise perfect superstars. I saw how pernicious such an ideation was—for both us and our children. For parents, this effort pushes us toward unrelenting control. We feel it is our duty to micromanage our children's every mood, choice, and behavior. This constant striving creates within us the onus to feel responsible for their every outcome. What pressure indeed! And if we feel this pressure, let's try to imagine what this pressure does to children who feel burdened by our obsession to excel, succeed, and "be happy"; what do we imagine our children feel when they realize they cannot be who it is they authentically need to be but instead must be an instrument for our well-being? How is this child supposed to feel safe and free to develop in tune with their own inner knowing? Impossible, isn't it?

Well, this is why the conscious parenting model debunks this entire delusion of parental control and challenges parents to burn it down. Conscious parenting understands that we as parents can be in charge of our children, for sure, but we cannot be in control of them. It reveals that no matter how "good" we try to be as parents, "bad" things can still happen to our children. Instead of shaming ourselves for these inevitabilities, conscious parenting teaches parents to connect to themselves and their children from a place of deep healing and empowerment. And Kristina's journey eloquently links the principles of conscious parenting with her lived experiences as a mother in real time.

Conscious parenting upholds that our children are on earth not to fulfill our fantasies and expectations but instead to live in a manner that is authentic to themselves—even if this looks contrary to our agenda for them. As parents learn to honor and celebrate their children for who they are and unconditionally accept them—no matter what they might be struggling with—the relationship between parent and child thrives. Of course, in order for the parent to arrive at such a place of emotional and psychological maturity, they need to have "raised themselves" into an inner state of acceptance and wholeness.

We parents don't realize how our actions of care and concern can actually feel stifling and controlling to our children. We believe we are acting in the best faith and are puzzled, even hurt, when our children don't receive our actions as such. They reject us and often withdraw from us—the very consequences we thought we would avoid with our "care." This causes us to be frustrated with them and lash out through blind reactivity. Inevitably, we arrive at an emotional impasse. Only when we are able to go inward and realize that much of our care and concern emerges from our own childhood fears around imperfection and unworthiness can we stop projecting our fears onto our children, which in turn releases them from the pressure to act in ways that make us feel better about ourselves. Instead of constantly feeling the burden of managing our expectations, our children can discover their desires and manage their own expectations.

Kristina's inner transformation articulately speaks to how the traditional parenting approach fueled by fear, shame, and control simply does not work and can in fact backfire and make family life much worse. When Kristina began to focus on her own inner healing, she was able to see her son with the empathy, sensitivity, and compassion he so desperately needed from her. While before she viewed his behaviors as being reflective of who she was as a mother—and therefore took things personally, causing her to be emotionally reactive—she later learned to separate her emotional state from her son's behavior. As she began to un-enmesh her identity as a mother from who her son was, she was able to actually see him in deep and profound ways. The more she was able to resist taking things personally, the more inner space she had to recognize and respect his needs with greater precision and care. The space to see clearly freed her from blindly reacting to him out of fear and from a place of powerlessness. She learned to inculcate the confidence to pause and allow him to experience all his feelings, even the ones that scared her. He felt safe. And just as all children do when they feel safe, he began to blossom.

Kristina's ability to share the darkest, most vulnerable moments on her son's path toward wholeness is the most rewarding element of this book. Because she takes us so deep into her private inner spaces and shows us their raw, unfinished, and imperfect crevices, she boldly normalizes those same spaces we hold within ourselves and don't dare reveal to the world. Because she so authentically exposes her own inner demons, she gives us the confidence to do the same. Our common humanity lies in our pain. I always say that pain is the greatest portal to our inner transformation and awakening. Tragically, most of us run away from the pain in our lives, burying it under addictions or distractions. Yet, when we accept pain, as Kristina did, we allow it to transform us and open ourselves to a greater sense of maturity, wisdom, and courage.

Let these pages lead you to a deeper place within your heart and soul as they did me. Thank you, Kristina. Thank you to your beautiful son, who shares his courage to heal. Such is the power of one mother's story of her darkest moments; she shines a torch during our own and allows us to find our way to light.

—Dr. Shefali Tsabary

I Can Fix This

Lie #1

I Can Fix This

———◇———

I'm looking straight at my son's face and yet I don't see him. I'm staring into his blue eyes, the eyes that have been so full of curiosity, full of laughter, full of energy and love, and yet somehow they're empty now. I see the bloody scabs on his knuckles. He's been punching the shower tiles again, trying to feel any pain other than the pain of depression and anxiety. I approach him slowly and wrap my arms around his body, now taller than mine, that same body that was placed in my arms fifteen years ago when he made me a mother for the first time. I hold him tightly, I can hear his breath, I can feel his heartbeat, yet he's not here. I want my son back.

———◇———

*L*uka, my firstborn, is the best surprise of my life. I was a year and a half into my marriage with his dad, and we were not planning on having children yet. Nevertheless, I found myself crouched in a closet on the phone with the nurse who'd given me a pregnancy test a few hours earlier. She tells me that I'm going to be a mother. Immediately the tears come. And so does the deep, deep love for this child I have yet to meet.

From his very first breath, Luka is like fire. He is luminous and bright, intense and playful, creative and funny, sensitive and warm, with a mind of his own, the courage to always express what is on the inside, and a stubbornness that I know will both hold him back and help him soar. From early on, I can sense that this child will teach me and challenge me, and I want to stay open.

Sometime between the ages of twelve and thirteen, I notice Luka's disposition and behavior start to change, and I quickly diagnose him with the common human condition known as: teenager. Apparently, 100 percent of human adults were at one point afflicted by this condition. He seems to have all the typical symptoms: decreased patience with family members; mood swings; rolling of the eyes; one-word answers to most questions; isolating in his room; a shift from goofy, fun, and talkative to serious, negative, and quiet; frequent annoyance with simple things like me standing in my kitchen, me complimenting him, me saying good morning to him; and a general irritability directed toward . . . me. All of me. Every. Bit. Of me. When it comes to patience, my strengths lie elsewhere. But luckily Luka's stepdad, my husband, Philip, is an overachiever in this area and I'm grateful he can help keep me centered.

None of this particularly worries me. I'm almost proud! Luka excels at being an adolescent.

I remember being his age, and I know that insecurities get much louder and aggressive in the teen years, so for Luka's thirteenth birthday I wake him up with breakfast in bed and a video I put together. It's a montage of all the important people in his life, one by one, saying something very specific they love about Luka. He sits in his bed eating Nutella-filled crepes and watching family members, friends, friends' parents, and former teachers all showering him with love and reminding him how amazing he is. I figure every human could use a video like this at least once a year, but especially a teenager.

Teenagers, the way I see it, are wearing a mask. It's not a mask they've put on willingly or can remove at their own whim. It's not a papier-mâché mask with fun, bright paint, but instead a mask made of hormones, complicated feelings, social pressures, insecurities, and stress. Underneath that mask is the child I know really well, the child with the same traits and the same heart that I've known for all the years I've nurtured and guided him, the child who, with each new year of his life, reveals to me more and more exactly who he is.

Eventually, after some potentially turbulent teen years, the mask will come off. I will then celebrate. Red carpet, tiara, and all the trophies in the world for having made it through that extra-, *extra*-special stage of parenting. Until then, all I have to do is:

1. For the sake of my sanity: remind myself at least sixty-four times a day that this phase will pass
2. For the sake of Luka's sanity: not rush him out of this phase

3. For the sake of everyone's sanity: put my child's needs before my and everyone else's unrealistic expectations

Easy (said no parent ever).

I really thought I'd be successful in raising teenagers. For a few years, straight out of college and before I had kids, I worked at a high school as an assistant theater director and occasionally substituted in various classes. I was in my early twenties, so because of the proximity in age with the students, and my playful personality, they felt very comfortable opening up to me and sharing personal struggles. I had so many deep conversations with these kids. I sat with a girl while she told me that she might be pregnant, that she was confused and terrified and didn't know how to tell anyone but me. I had long conversations with various students who shared with me their stories of being bullied or pressured into activities they didn't want to partake in, or struggling with an eating disorder, or living in a home full of chaos where the parents behaved as if they hated each other. I saw the stress and fear and pressure these students felt on a daily basis. I witnessed their extreme mood swings. I learned how much they just wanted to be seen and heard and valued.

I have deep compassion for kids that age, because I had a hard time as a teenager. My family moved to the US from

Croatia during the war there, when I was fourteen years old. Beyond all the typical teen insecurities and stress, I was also adjusting to a completely different culture and a completely different standard of what was cool and what wasn't. I was trying to communicate my thoughts and feelings in a foreign language when I didn't even know how to communicate my thoughts and feelings clearly in my native tongue, in a private diary. I was struggling to make friends who would be patient with me during my adjustment period, and on top of all that and more, I was feeling guilty that I got to leave war-torn Croatia while my friends were stuck back there. Everything felt complicated and messy and too much, and I felt misunderstood and lost and not enough.

During those years, I felt anxious or depressed more often than I allowed people to see, but I didn't even have the words for what I was grappling with back then. In the 1990s, I didn't know anyone who openly discussed depression or anxiety or any type of mental health struggle. I don't even remember hearing those words said out loud. If mental health was ever brought up, it was always in the context of *those crazy people who need to be locked up in a psych ward.*

We were all just considered screwed-up teenagers with screwed-up feelings we'd eventually grow out of. I'm not sure if a doctor would've diagnosed me with depression and anxiety, or if what I experienced was any more extreme than the average nineties teen, but I wonder how different my experience of young adulthood could have been if I had been in therapy. What if, at the time, I had someone who could have helped me process and organize the mess in my head, and validate all my weird emotions as normal ones? I've always felt like the world would be a better place if every human were assigned a therapist right at birth. You enter the world, and before they even cut the umbilical cord or place the hospital ID bracelet around your chubby little ankle, they hand you a business card. "Here's your therapist's number. Use as needed. In other words, use often."

So going into motherhood, I felt like my own experiences and my empathy for teenagers in general gave me a leg up in the parenting game. I genuinely believed that I would be at least average, but most likely way above average (maybe even valedictorian status), when it came to knowing exactly how to handle and support my children once they reached those intense years.

But there's a big difference between working with teenagers and parenting your own teenager.

How does a mother, especially with her very first child, know when her kid is experiencing "normal" teenage hormones and when there's something more serious at hand? It would be wonderful if children, or humans in general, were equipped with the ability to clearly assess and express all their feelings, thoughts, struggles, and needs, and even better if we, as their loved ones, could immediately understand and instantly know how to fix it all. But that's a fantasy that has never and will never exist.

Here's how parenting Luka at this age looks from my end: We give him privileges. He betrays our trust. So we take away some of those privileges, which leaves him feeling trapped. With time, we slowly reintroduce some of the privileges, explaining that he can have even more freedom when he shows us that he's trustworthy. He agrees, but then quickly betrays our trust again. And so the cycle continues. Fun, fun for everyone.

And I'm just going about my parenting, thinking that my kid is simply more teenagery than most teenagers.

As the cycle we're stuck in grows more intense and wears us out, it starts feeling like denial and fear are each campaigning for my vote. They are opposing candidates, with very different views on what's best for everyone involved, and each is trying to convince me to side with them.

Denial's main campaign message is: It's not that serious. Most teenagers act like this and eventually grow out of it.

Denial's slogan is: Don't panic. This too shall pass.

Fear's campaign message is: THIS IS THE WORST POSSIBLE THING THAT COULD HAPPEN IN ALL OF THE UNIVERSE!

Fear's slogan is: PANIC, PANIC, PANIC!

And I'm the undecided voter who thinks both opponents seem a little unstable. I find myself agreeing with Denial one second and the next feeling very strongly that Fear will lead to more progress.

Luka stops turning in school assignments and starts failing classes in subjects that he thrived in just a semester ago.

Denial: School is hard at this age. He just needs a tutor to help him out every once in a while.

Fear: ALERT. ALERT. ALERT. THE KID IS FAILING! GET STRICTER OR HE'LL END UP LIVING ON THE STREETS SOMEDAY!

Luka buys a vape from a kid at school.

Denial: It's just nicotine. Teenagers and smoking? Not really breaking news. He's simply testing boundaries, experimenting with something forbidden, imitating what other kids his age are doing.

Fear: WHO IS HE? THIS IS NOT THE SON YOU RAISED! YOU'VE TALKED TO HIM ABOUT VAPING FROM A YOUNG AGE. YOU MUST PANIC! AND THEN PANIC SOME MORE. AND THEN GARNISH THAT WITH A HUGE DOLLOP OF FRESH PANIC.

He starts hanging out with the type of people he didn't respect before and becomes super focused on fitting in with them.

Denial: Normal.

Fear: HE'S GOING TO END UP IN PRISON!

He starts lying daily.

He stops taking care of his responsibilities.

He's regularly late to his classes.

He's being disrespectful to his teachers.

He stops obeying our rules.

He stops obeying school rules.

He seems to have lost all empathy for others.

He's become meaner and meaner to his sister.

He stops taking any accountability for his actions.

He starts blaming everyone else for his actions.

His attitude toward me escalates into lashing out in furious outbursts.

His tutor quits.

The tutor who we were PAYING A GENERGOUS AMOUNT OF COLD HARD CASH QUITS, because . . . (please refer to the preceding list).

And through every single new change, Denial is screaming: He's a typical teenager! And Fear keeps interrupting Denial with: THIS IS GOING TO END VERY, VERY BADLY UNLESS WE NIP THINGS IN THE BUD RIGHT NOW AND SEIZE CONTROL!

I'm too flustered trying to figure out who to cast my vote

for, or to even think clearly and productively, so I don't recognize that neither candidate is proposing a policy that will
actually lead to real change.

Without realizing it, I am choosing not to learn. I'm allowing the symptoms of my son's situation to distract me from
searching for the root of the problem.

Now, if someone had approached me at the time and told
me I was refusing to learn, I would have quickly dismissed the
accusation and in a very defensive tone replied, "I know the
importance of paying attention and choosing to continually
learn new ways to support and guide my children. I am always
open to learning, thank you very much!"

But we aren't open to learning if we've already decided we
know what the problem is, and how to solve it. In my mind,
the "problem" was a rebellious teenager, and the solution was
to love him through it, remind him of his strengths, all while
still giving him guidelines and responsibilities so that he
could grow into a mature, kind, confident, self-sufficient adult.

But even with the best of intentions, I still came at Luka
from a place of assumption, instead of a place of curiosity.

This is one of my first big mistakes in trying to support
Luka.

An assumption is a period, or even worse, an exclamation
point. It requires only one participant. There's a finality to it.
The sentence has been spoken. It is what it is.

Curiosity is a genuine question mark. It requires explora-
tion. It requires thought. It requires patience. It requires a response. It's a dance between the one who holds the interest
and the one who holds the revelation.

Assumption is, often unintentionally, led by ego and inse-
curity and the need to stay comfortable.

Curiosity is intentionally led by pure love and awe and the
courage to get very, very uncomfortable.

Where we trick ourselves with curiosity is in thinking that
simply adding question marks to the ends of our sentences
makes us curious. The question mark becomes like an acces-
sory, the workout outfit I put on, even though I don't actually
go to the gym. The question mark makes me feel like I'm
being attentive and proactive and choosing to learn, but my
questions are obscured by so many assumptions and precon-
ceived answers that there's really no room for any learning to
get through.

True curiosity, as my friend Jason puts it, means standing
in awe of someone's story.

I am not standing in awe of Luka's story. I am simply ob-
serving the surface level and reacting.

My questions sound like: What's going on with you that
you're suddenly failing classes? What do you need from me in
order to get your act together? Why are you late again? How
can I help you stop behaving like this? What can I do to help

you get off this dangerous path you're on? Why are you not using the intelligence and common sense that I know you have? Why don't you care?

His answers sound like: I don't know. Nothing. Whatever. Leave me alone.

My questions seem reasonable to me at the time, but each of them screams, "You're not good enough." Feeling like a loser has never helped anyone thrive. I know this, but I don't see it in this moment.

My questions are filled with judgment. His answers are filled with withdrawal.

I am not standing in awe of Luka's story.

An occasional good day and Denial sways me to its side. On a more frequent bad day, I'm spiraling into Fear's scariest what-ifs. I swing from one extreme to the other, feeling disoriented and dizzy, and eventually everything starts feeling completely out of control.

I decide to find Luka a therapist.

After doing a lot of research, I email a highly recommended therapist in our area and he replies to let me know that he is at capacity and not taking any new clients. He has a referral he'd like to recommend, though it comes with a small caveat. The therapist he can refer us to has his master's degree in marriage and family therapy and is nearing completion of the three thousand in-session hours required for licensure. But he isn't licensed yet. This therapist can offer his services more as a life coach. His name is Tim and he's great with teens and has a wealth of experience working with them.

After my divorce years ago, and all the drama and struggles that followed, I sank into a pretty dark place and couldn't afford therapy, so I started attending sessions with a psychology grad student who needed to log treatment hours. It was a very positive experience for me, so I decide that we should give Tim a try.

I first schedule a session alone with Tim so that I can get a sense of his approach and give him some background information, because at this point I'm not sure how honest or open Luka is willing to be.

Luka is fourteen at the time and thinks seeing a life coach/therapist is my way of punishing him for the disrespect and vaping and all the complaints I'm getting from his school.

"But I think it would be really helpful for you to have someone to talk to, Luka."

"I have my friends to talk to."

"Well, it helps to have someone who is objective. And not a kid. Trust me, this will be good for you. You get to express whatever you need to express. You even get to complain about me and I won't even know it."

Luka still sees therapy as a punishment, and though I know I can get him to the appointment, I also know that no one can force him to talk if he decides not to participate.

Tim does an excellent job bonding with Luka in the first session. They spend pretty much the entire fifty minutes just talking about video games. I'm feeling that my money is probably being wasted, but hoping this approach will lead to Luka opening up.

In the following weeks and months, my hope begins to dissipate as Luka is getting worse, not better. His attitude toward me has reached a level that feels like emotional abuse, emails from frustrated teachers are now popping up regularly in my inbox, and I'm growing incredibly frustrated that I'm not seeing any progress from Luka's weekly sessions with Tim.

Late one night, I start searching the internet for camps for troubled teenagers. Some are boot camps that use a strict military-inspired approach to teach teens discipline and whip their attitude into shape. Others are wilderness camps that promise a peaceful, restorative environment where teens will be completely removed from any negative influences so that they can finally experience emotional healing and maturity. All promise that by the time the kids leave camp, even the most treatment-resistant and rebellious adolescents will be transformed. The websites feature quotes from parents thanking the camps for their brand-spanking new and improved child. There are photos of smiling teenagers riding horses, exercising at sunrise, and cooking dinner together. It's all very enticing, especially to a mother who is completely and utterly exhausted and wishes there was a wilderness camp she could ship her own ass to right now. But something in my gut keeps me from filling out an inquiry form.

One day, after yet another email from a disappointed teacher and yet another angry outburst during the conversation about said email, I tell Luka that he is grounded from hanging out with friends and grounded from playing videos games until further notice. I'm expecting this announcement to lead to more rage from him, but instead he calmly says, "Okay."

I figure he'll eventually come to me, as he always does, and try to talk me into changing my mind and decreasing his punishment, but he doesn't. Hours go by, days go by, and not once does he ask for leniency like he used to. He doesn't seem to care. He used to care.

I slowly start noticing that the same apathy Luka has about his consequences, he seems to have for everything else in his life. Of all the parts of his life that once brought him joy—his friends, sports, various activities and hobbies and games—none of them are bringing him joy anymore. He's not just isolating from his parents like many teenagers do, he is isolating from everyone and everything he used to love and care about. This doesn't strike me as typical teenage hormones.

I book a solo session with Tim. As I sit down on the sofa across from his chair, in the small, badly lit room, I suddenly realize that I'm not even sure why I'm there. I don't know what I need or what I want or what I should say or ask. I just know that I don't know.

"I understand that unless Luka is threatening to do something dangerous, you're not supposed to share with me what you talk about in your sessions with him, and that's fine. What I'm wondering is . . . I guess . . . I don't know. I'm wondering if there's something I'm missing. Something important. Something deeper than him just being rebellious."

"Clinical depression?" Tim asks.

I look at him and freeze. *Clinical depression.* Those words feel so heavy. Too heavy for a boy who, until recently, seemed so light and playful and free.

Tim continues, "I've been thinking about this for a little while, but I'm not licensed and should not be diagnosing clients, so instead, how about I read to you the symptoms of major depressive disorder and then we can discuss?"

He pulls a textbook from the shelf behind his chair. The book is titled *Abnormal Psychology.* I immediately hate the person who came up with that title. Tim flips through the pages until he lands on the one he's looking for, and he begins to read: "If a person is experiencing some of the following signs and symptoms most of the day, nearly every day, for at least two weeks, they may be suffering from depression. Some people experience only a few symptoms, while others may experience many. Several persistent symptoms in addition to low mood are required for a diagnosis of major depression."

Tim starts reading the symptoms.

Persistent sad, anxious, or "empty" mood

Feelings of hopelessness or pessimism

Irritability

Loss of interest or pleasure in hobbies and activities

After each symptom Tim reads, he glances up at me with a look of "yep." And with each new glance, my eyes well up more and more, because . . . yep.

"Feelings of guilt, worthlessness, or helplessness."

Yep.

"Decreased energy or fatigue."

Yep.

"Moving or talking more slowly."

Yep.

"Feeling restless or having trouble sitting still."

Yep.

"Difficulty concentrating, remembering, or making decisions."

Yep.

"Difficulty sleeping, early-morning awakening, or over-sleeping."

Yep.

"Thoughts of death or suicide, or suicide attempts."

Oh God, I hope not. I hope not.

At this point my face is drenched with tears, and my mind is as blurry as my vision. Except for one crystal-clear thought: I failed my boy.

I Am in Control

———◇———

Five-year-old Luka leans in. His eyes are red, his hands shaky.

I had just taken him and his younger sister to see the animated movie *Up*. In short, the movie is about an elderly man named Carl who (spoiler alert) loses his beloved wife in the first five minutes of the movie, a young Boy Scout named Russell who misses his dad since his parents' divorce, and their crazy adventure, which includes thousands of balloons, a talking dog, and profound themes that leave the viewer feeling all the feels.

After the movie, as we are walking to the parking lot, Luka is not his usual talkative self—the boy eager to excitedly recount his favorite parts. He is completely silent. We get in the car, and he immediately starts sobbing. His hands shake as he leans toward me.

"Oh, buddy, is it the movie?"

Luka nods.

"Because Carl's wife died? Or the boy's dad not having time for him?"

Luka looks up at me, his face covered in tears, his lips quivering. "It's because . . . it's because people are so lonely. The old man was lonely and the boy was lonely, and so many people in the world are very lonely. I don't want anyone to feel so lonely."

I am stunned at his deep empathy and love.

Now, fourteen-year-old Luka leans in. His eyes are red, his hands are shaky.

I have just picked him up from school. When we arrive home, he heads straight to his room to check if I have once again searched it. I have. While he was at school, I confiscated yet another vape. Even though he was recently diagnosed with asthma that's been caused by vaping, he still won't give it up. Now he comes running downstairs and confronts me.

"I hate you, you fucking bitch!" he screams in my face, then punches a hole in the wall and storms off.

I am stunned at his deep animosity and aggression.

What did I do wrong? How does a child with such a tender heart turn into a child so full of hatred?

*T*he day after my one-on-one meeting with Tim, I'm in the car with Luka, driving home from who knows where, doing who knows what. I don't know it yet, but this is going to be one of those days when I experience a pivotal moment so big, it erases all other moments of that day from memory.

"Luka . . . I need to ask you something and I need you to be completely honest with me. Okay?"

He nods.

"Have you ever thought about hurting yourself?"

Even though I'm the one asking the question, I suddenly feel like I've fallen off the trail of my regular life and into a deep pit of lava. My body is so attuned to what Luka might say next that I feel hot and uneasy. I'm hoping he'll issue a confident "No, never!" and am dreading any other response. But more than anything, I need the absolute truth from him.

The short pause between my question and his answer feels like a lifetime.

His head drops down. Very calmly and quietly he replies, "Yes."

Yes. My child has thought about hurting himself.

I start to panic, and suddenly it feels like an emotional bodyguard is right behind me, grasping my arms, trying to hold me back from succumbing to my fear, whispering in my ear, "Okay, that's enough for today. No more questions."

But I push forward.

"When you have those thoughts, is it because you want to die?"

"Sometimes."

"Have you ever tried to . . . ?"

"No. Not yet."

Not yet. Yet. Yet. Yet. Everything feels . . . not real. I have forgotten how to breathe or string words into sentences. I feel devastated and scared and unequipped.

In the bigness of this moment, I have an impulse—which I'm sure many humans would have—to quickly right the ship. I want to say, "You don't really want to hurt yourself. You don't really want to die. I'm sure you don't! You have so much good in your life!" As a mother, I so passionately want to convince my child that he doesn't really mean what he's saying, and to somehow, immediately, shut down those dark thoughts he's having. But when my child tells me, "I feel *this*," if my reply is, "No, you don't really feel *this*," I'm betraying the truth of his experience. Why would my child ever open up to me again? And even worse, could that kind of reaction push my child toward desperately trying to prove to me that he wants to die?

Fear has completely hijacked my brain, but the only thing I know for sure in this moment is that I need my kid to keep talking to me, because I can't help him without the gift he just gave me of his truth and vulnerability.

So I take a deep breath. I don't scream or sob, I just keep this hard conversation going. "Buddy, I am so sorry. I am so, so sorry that you have these thoughts. And I'm sorry I didn't know. I'm sorry I didn't ask until now. I love you so much and I am going to figure out what we can do to help you feel better. Luka, I want you here."

I spend the next day trying to get referrals for a psychiatrist who specializes in treating adolescents. Three weeks later (because nothing regarding mental health is immediate, including getting an appointment), we're meeting with a highly recommended psychiatrist.

She's in her sixties and looks like the type of person who would offer us a cup of tea and homemade banana bread if we were walking into her living room instead of walking into her psychiatric office.

The appointment is long and very thorough. I'm thankful that she's given us so much time. The doctor speaks first with both of us together, then with Luka alone, and then it's my turn to go in alone.

"Ms. Kuzmič, your son is severely depressed. I don't say this lightly and I'm not one to prescribe medication to children unless I find it absolutely necessary, but in Luka's case, I would feel very concerned if we tried to manage this without the help of an antidepressant. I will bring him back in, we can discuss the options together and all the possible side effects. Ultimately it's your decision. I also need you to know that I only prescribe medication to kids who are in weekly therapy, and I know he's been seeing someone, but it's time to find a licensed therapist."

As much as giving children psychotropic medications makes me nervous, I trust that this is the right decision for Luka, and I'm eager for him to start feeling better. Sometimes all of the processing and support isn't enough. The depression is so strong that a person is unable to apply all that they've learned. It's like knowing how to swim, maybe even being an excellent swimmer, but the current is so powerful that despite all your efforts you can't make any headway. Medication calms the current. Therapy helps you swim forward.

During the ride home, Luka doesn't say anything. After some time, I ask, "How do you feel about what the doctor said?"

"I don't know. Weird, I guess."

"The feeling of depression is weird or the diagnosis of depression is weird?"

"The diagnosis. It's not normal. I'm not normal."

I feel protective of my son and angry at the big, bad world that still paints mental health struggles as not normal. I tell him that considering how heavy life is and how complicated human beings are with all our genetic predispositions mixed with the unpredictable circumstances thrown our way, in my opinion, what doesn't seem normal is feeling 100 percent mentally healthy. Struggling seems normal. Confusion seems normal. Complicated feelings seem normal. Needing help seems normal. He isn't broken. The system is broken. The lack of emphasis on mental health—that's what's broken.

"Luka, when you've had a really bad cold, I would give you some medication to help you feel better. You never thought that was weird, because it wasn't. It's not. Now you have depression, so we'll give you some medication to help you feel better. I don't want you to think that's weird, because it's not."

The next few weeks are rough. We are told that with antidepressants, people sometimes start feeling worse before they start feeling better. The thoughts of suicide could increase before they decrease.

I am living in constant fear.

Luka starts seeing a licensed therapist named Brian, who has years of experience working with teenagers who struggle with mental illness, and he encourages Luka to assume responsibility for his choices, rather than use depression as an excuse. He is empathetic but firm. Luka doesn't enjoy going to therapy, but he doesn't fight me on it too much. Each time I write a check for therapy, I think about my life a decade prior. I had no money. I was on food stamps. I shared a small bedroom with my children. If I was in that same financial position now, how could I afford to help Luka? Even with great insurance, so much goes uncovered. I'm grateful for all of the access I have now and heartbroken for any parent who can't afford the support their family deserves. I'm disgusted by this system that's failing so many people.

Things at home with Luka are still very, very chaotic.

One night, Luka has a couple of friends sleep over. After we go to bed, he and his friends sneak some alcohol, and Luka gets drunk for the first time. He's fifteen, everyone else is drinking, so he does too. And in that drunk state, he finds he is once again full of life. The funny, outgoing, charismatic, happy Luka is back for a few hours.

The antidepressant isn't an instant, magical cure for Luka. Therapy isn't an instant, magical cure. But the alcohol sure seems like it might be.

I once met an older gentleman who described his attraction to alcohol in a way that contextualized the seduction so well: He told me the story of really struggling when he was a kid, full of insecurities, sad and anxious. He compared it to feeling like a duck, like a weak, little, awkward duck. One day, he opened a kitchen cabinet and found a bottle of alcohol that belonged to his dad. He twisted open the cap, didn't like the smell, but decided to take a big swig of it anyway. Then he took another swig. And another. Soon he noticed that he no longer felt like a weak, little, awkward duck. For the first time ever, he felt like an eagle. A big, powerful, invincible eagle. Why would anyone want to feel like a frail duck when they can feel like a mighty eagle?

The problem with this magical transformation is that pulling it off always requires more—more alcohol, more experimentation, more secrets. Luka's next instant, magical cure comes from trying marijuana—often laced with something far more dangerous. And eventually from the prescription pain pills that he gets from kids at school. Luka is now happy only if he is drunk or high or both, and soon the only reason he shows up to school is to get alcohol and drugs from kids who are willing to share. The only time he makes plans with people is when he knows they have alcohol or drugs. His entire existence becomes about figuring out the next time he can get intoxicated.

So every morning after he leaves for school, I search his

room. More often than not, I find some sort of drug paraphernalia or an empty bottle of alcohol under his bed or hidden in his dresser drawers.

One day I find a ziplock bag full of sugar under his sink. I'm perplexed. But then I figure out that he's pouring the sugar into the bottle of wine to help it go down easier. Being intoxicated has become less about feeling familiar to himself and more about numbing the pain altogether.

Philip, my husband, and I remove all alcohol from the house, but not before Luka manages to find and finish the special bottle of wine we had saved from our wedding day.

His lying intensifies. There is more to lie about now.

When kids at school get sick of sharing their stash with him, Luka starts stealing from us to buy his own stash, and eventually starts selling drugs to kids at school, even tricking people into buying broken drug paraphernalia from him, in order to be able to afford more drugs.

He becomes increasingly hostile to anyone who stands between him and his coping mechanisms of choice. The outbursts that started when he was first depressed and showed up as disrespectfully talking back to me turn into rage that leads to doors slamming in my face, holes punched in the walls, broken furniture, and furious explosions so intense that my mind goes blank.

An email shows up in my inbox. It's from the high school principal to all parents, informing us that an ambulance was called to the school that afternoon to take two girls to the hospital. Apparently they were smoking pot at lunch, but it was laced with something that caused them to have seizures. No other information is shared. I panic. I hope the girls will be okay, and also hope that this incident will scare Luka. I try to bring it up as soon as he's home from school, but he cuts me off. "Mom, I know. I heard. It's not that big of a deal. You're so dramatic."

I have completely lost control of my child. I don't even feel like I know him anymore. I start reading books about raising teenagers who are struggling and get checklists of recommendations.

Communicate openly with your teenager. Check.

Put your teen in individual therapy. Check.

Book family therapy sessions. Check.

Eat dinner together as a family. Check.

Encourage your teen in their strengths and talents. Check.

Put in writing simple expectations your child needs to meet each day (e.g., brush their teeth, show up to school). Check.

Make a big deal when your child meets even the smallest expectation. Check.

If need be, have your child see a psychiatrist. Check.

Compliment your child often. Check.

Establish appropriate rules, boundaries, and consequences. Check.

Remind your child every day, regardless of their behavior, how much you love them. Check.

But nothing seems to work. I now reside full time in the waiting/hoping state. If the doctor adjusts Luka's medication again, maybe he'll feel better. If he has more time in therapy, things will improve. If the next few months bring a little more maturity, everything will start heading in a more positive direction. If I can learn not to be so reactive to his negative attitude, our relationship will be stronger.

If. If. If.

Mental health medication is complicated. What works for one person might not work for another. It's a trial-and-error process, and it can take time. At one of the psychiatry appointments, the doctor suggests weaning Luka off the current antidepressant and trying a different one. I am once again hopeful. After meeting with Luka alone for longer than I expected, the doctor pulls me out of the waiting room to speak with me privately. Her usual sweet, gentle smile has been replaced with a look of complete frustration. "I won't be able to adjust his medication. I told him that he needs to stop using drugs for at least a few weeks so that we can clearly assess how the new medication is affecting his system and whether it's working. His reply to me was a defiant no. I asked if he could give me just two weeks. He said no. I am not putting him on medication when I don't even know exactly what type of pills he's getting from kids each day or what the marijuana he's using might be laced with. My hands are tied."

On the way home, I beg Luka to please do what his psychiatrist asked him to do. I know he wants to feel better and I need him to believe that a different medication might make a difference. But Luka is just pissed at the doctor for sharing with me what they talked about in private. He feels betrayed and tells me that he is never going back to her again.

Luka feels that life would be better and simpler if the adults in his life would just stop ganging up on him. If his parents weren't so strict. If everyone would just back off and let him live his life his way.

If. If. If.

A few weeks later, on my father-in-law's birthday, we plan a big family dinner at an upscale restaurant in a nearby town.

Luka has tutoring that evening. It is the third time we have tried tutoring for him. The first tutor quit, and the second couldn't make any progress with him. I'm not trying to get this kid to any specific grade point average, I'm just trying to get him to graduation. I know he's capable. He went from being on the honor roll one year to failing classes the next.

Because I don't want Luka to miss tutoring, I tell everyone else to head over to dinner without us, and I'll come with Luka once he's done. We'll be only a few minutes late.

During this tense period of our lives, most of my interactions with Luka start the same way. I make a very conscious decision that I will approach him with calmness. I will remain calm for our entire exchange. I will find something positive to say. I won't let him get to me. I am calm. Calmness is me.

I have the same lovely intentions that day.

Luka gets in the car and says, "You're wasting your money on tutoring. I don't even give a shit about any of it, and I'm going to drop out of school anyway." The calmness starts leaking out of my body right away. We are less than a minute into this interaction, and I am already not feeling calm. Calmness is not me. Instead of arguing, I try to find something positive to say. I blurt out, "You're smarter than that." (Which is really another way of saying, "You're being stupid." So not quite the positive remark I'm aiming for.) He counters with a complaint about my rules, and instead of just letting him talk, I interrupt him to point out how thoughtful and sensible my rules actually are. I can't resist responding to his every argument, as if my responses can safeguard him against making mistakes. I fall into the trap of explaining and defending myself instead of really hearing him, and *boom*, the fight escalates.

"You're a horrible fucking mother!" Luka says with anger.

"Do not talk to me like that," I say firmly.

His voice gets louder. "You're a bitch. You're the worst piece of shit mother and you never should have had kids!"

"Luka, you need to take a breath and stop talking right now."

34

At this point, I'm pulling into the parking lot of the restaurant and just as I park the car, he adds, "Next time use a condom!"

I turn to him and, without any thought, I slap him right across the face. I slap him really hard.

We both freeze for a split second, and then he opens the car door and runs.

I didn't mean to hit him. My body just reacted. All the patience had been squeezed out of me. All the words were used up, and I snapped.

I have never spanked my children, not once, not even a little swat on the butt when they were young. Their dad and I decided before we ever had kids that we wouldn't spank for a variety of reasons, one being that we didn't want to send our kids the message that the way you get someone to respect you or listen to you is by physically hurting them.

Now, without ever having laid a hand on Luka before, I have completely lost control and I have slapped him across the face.

As he runs off, I burst into tears and immediately call Philip. "I need you to leave the restaurant and talk to me outside. Right now, please. Quickly."

Philip excuses himself from the table and runs outside. "I hit him. I hit him hard. I slapped him. And he ran away. I don't know where he went but I'm scared he's going to hurt himself."

"Stay here. I'll look for him."

Philip leaves me in the car, and I watch him jog across the

parking lot. Within a few minutes, he spots Luka ahead of him and catches up. Luka is sobbing. He looks at Philip and through tears angrily says, "I'm a mistake. I'm a fucking failure and I shouldn't even be here."

I'm not sure exactly how Philip responded in that moment, but he shines in these tense situations, and he has a way of connecting with Luka to defuse the situation without ignoring the gravity of Luka's emotions.

About ten minutes later, Philip calls to tell me that they are walking back toward the restaurant. I meet them near the entrance. Luka's face is red from crying. I am still crying. My voice trembles but there are things I know I can't leave unsaid, even for the next hour. "I want to apologize to you for hitting you. I want to apologize for completely losing control. I do not for one second condone the way you spoke to me. It was beyond disrespectful; it was vulgar. It was wrong! However, hitting you was not the correct way to handle that, and I am sorry."

I am hoping Luka will apologize as well, or at least say that he understands why I reacted the way I did, but he says nothing.

The last thing I want to do in this moment is walk into that restaurant, sit at a birthday dinner, and pretend everything is fine. But I tell Luka that I'd really like to set this aside for a few hours so that we can show up for his grandpa and celebrate him. He nods in agreement.

As the three of us walk toward the beautifully set table in the corner of the dining room, we probably look like we just escaped a zombie apocalypse.

The waiter approaches to take my order and I point to the first thing I see on the menu. I'm worried if I try to speak, my voice will give way to crying. My mother-in-law reaches over and touches my hand. She whispers, "Are you okay?" I nod. But the tears, like from a broken faucet, keep slowly dripping. As hard as I try to stop them, I can't.

The tears aren't just about the slap or even Luka's behavior. The broken faucet is a combination of feeling helpless and desperate; emotionally exhausted from trying so many different ways to make progress but seeing none, from fearing what's to come; and feeling completely lost as to what the next steps should be.

I can't help but think how different this dinner would have been if I had just not reacted to him. I gave in to my ego and fear, which intensified my need to control, which led me to react. I need to be emotionally available, not emotionally reactive. I know this. And yet once again I failed to put my best intentions into practice. The concept seems simple, but behaving rationally when I've been triggered feels impossible. Not reacting may not have changed his behavior, but it would have changed mine, and that's the only thing I actually have control over: me. If I can't control myself and be the steady adult in the room, we are doomed. Unless I have sure footing, I cannot weather this storm.

As I'm sitting at dinner, my mind racing, I realize that I've been expecting Luka to do something I can't even do: control his frustrations when I can't control mine. Beyond just being steady, consistent, and a loving support system for him, my job is also to model for him how to behave when things get loud and messy and painful. My modeling sucks right now.

Whenever I get completely overwhelmed by anxiety, my world feels dark and hopeless—unless and until I do something proactive. Sitting at that birthday dinner with an untouched plate of chicken piccata in front of me, and my husband desperately trying to make small talk so this dinner seems celebratory despite the obvious dark cloud, the only proactive thing I can think to do is to email Luka's therapist. I pull my cell phone out, hold it on my lap, under the table, and send Brian an email telling him what happened and asking for some guidance.

Brian calls me later that evening. I'm at home, it's late, and I appreciate him taking the time to talk to me. After a long conversation, he suggests Luka and I meet with him together. It won't be the first time we've done this, and our past joint sessions have been helpful for me. Before hanging up he says,

"Remember, every behavior is an attempt to communicate a want or a need. Luka's behavior is completely unacceptable, but it is not personal."

It's good to know, but it doesn't help me sleep much that night. My mind refuses to rest.

Over the next few days, when I share the slap story with a few people in my inner circle, more than one of them react with some version of, "Well, maybe that's exactly what he needed! Something to shock him, teach him a lesson, put him in his place."

This doesn't sit well with me.

How do you shock someone out of mental illness? That slap won't stop his aggression toward me. It will only make him hate himself even more, which will then lead to more aggression. The slap won't teach him a lesson. You can't punish or intimidate or scare someone out of depression.

When Luka is screaming at me, what is he actually saying?

I'm realizing that I have to learn a new language so that I can interpret what Luka is communicating to me, a language that's ever changing, and completely indistinguishable unless I am calm and not reactive. And when I feel the urge to react, can I learn to react to the actual problem instead of the symptoms? It's like focusing all my energy trying to clear the smoke billowing out from under the hood of a car and ultimately making no progress. I can do my best to try to get rid of the smoke, but unless I look deeper and try to figure out why the engine is on fire in the first place, the problem will not only continue but also get worse. Reacting to Luka calling me a bitch is a lot different than addressing the pain behind the comment.

Now, in any other situation, if I were treated this way, I would immediately remove the person from my life and never look back. Mental health struggles do not give anyone the right to emotionally abuse someone. "Hurt people hurt people" might be an explanation, but it is not a justification.

However, I am dealing with my minor child, who I am responsible for. I am not willing to remove him from my life right now. This doesn't mean the behavior should be overlooked and ignored; it means the root of the problem should not be overlooked and ignored. It's not about sending him the message that his behavior is acceptable or excusable, but making sure that the louder message, always, is that I care what's behind the behavior and I want to help.

While the words coming out of his mouth are "I hate you, you fucking bitch," what he is actually screaming at me is "Help me, Mom. I hate myself, and I want to die."

Leaning in. Eyes red. Hands shaky. I have so much to learn.

Lie #3

It's All My Fault

---○---

One evening when Luka is about a year and a half old and I'm very pregnant with Matea, their dad and I host a game night at our place with some friends. While we're all focused on another round of Dutch Blitz, I'm also keeping tabs on Luka, who is running around the kitchen with a portable phone in his hand, pressing buttons and excitedly talking in his cute gibberish, pretending he's on an important call. A few minutes later, we hear police sirens and wonder what is happening in our quiet little neighborhood. Then our doorbell rings, followed by a heavy knock. I waddle over, open the front door, and see two police officers on my doorstep.

"Ma'am, is everything okay?" one of the officers asks while trying to look past me into the house.

Confused, I reply, "Ummm . . . yes. Everything is good. What is this about?"

"Ma'am, can you please fully open the door so that we can look around?"

"Sure, but could you please tell me what this is about?"

"There was a call from this residence. The dispatcher had a long, unintelligible conversation with a young child. We need to look inside."

My son had accidentally called the cops on me. We tell this amusing story for years around the dinner table and it never fails to get a laugh.

What I don't know then is that years later, I will have to call the cops on my son.

My call isn't accidental. My call is deliberate. And it crushes me.

ate one night about a month after my father-in-law's not-so-festive birthday dinner, Luka is pacing the kitchen in an extremely agitated state. He is angry one second, then smiling and laughing and joking the next. He is moving quickly, back and forth, from the table to the refrigerator to the counter, and so on. He takes a lighter out of the kitchen drawer and says it might be fun to burn things. I grab the lighter from him.

"Luka, let's sit down. How about I get you a glass of water and you sit down?"

He turns on the gas stove and lights a piece of paper on fire. I quickly snatch it from him and throw it in the sink. After some more pacing, he grabs wood skewers from a drawer and starts lighting those. Again, I rush to take them from him. Luka says in a sort of joking but also matter-of-fact way that it might be fun to burn the house down. Philip is sleeping, but I call to him to wake him up and tell him to come downstairs. I'm not sure if Luka is on some sort of drug that is causing him to behave this way or if his behavior is part of a mental health issue that hasn't been addressed yet. I'm not even completely sure that this strange behavior isn't just an act to get a rise out of me. Philip and I try to get him to sit down and take a breath, but Luka won't stop pacing. He seems delirious. I ask him if he slept at all the night before. He comments that sleep is overrated. More pacing. Then he shuts himself in the small pantry. I open the door and find him crying. I get him to come out and he's back to pacing and threatening, then silly dancing, then crying again. Eventually, he exhausts himself, goes to his room, and falls asleep. I check on him throughout the night, every hour.

The next day, I call Brian, his therapist. He tells me that if I am ever in a situation where I'm worried Luka might hurt himself or someone else, or he is making any sort of threats, I should immediately call the police.

Have we really gotten to the point where I need to call the police on my child? How have things gotten so out of control when so much attention and help and support have been poured on this kid?

What. More. Can. I. Do?

The next day and in the following weeks, Luka doesn't exhibit that strange behavior again. He dismisses me when I try to get more information from him about that evening.

Two months pass, and my ex-husband is bringing Luka back from spending the weekend with him at his parents' house. When they arrive, Luka's dad immediately asks him to tell me what happened the night before. Luka doesn't speak. So his dad proceeds to tell me that he took a vape from Luka. After several minutes of trying unsuccessfully to retrieve the vape from his dad, Luka started to get violent. He began charging at him, attempting to knock him over. It was close to one a.m., and his dad worried all the noise and aggression would wake up everyone else in the house, so he ran outside, knowing Luka would follow. Outside, Luka continued trying to fight him, telling him that he needed the vape back because he owed someone twenty-five dollars for it. He said he was planning on stealing money from family members or even robbing a 7-Eleven in order to settle all his debts, because otherwise he could get beat up for not repaying the people he owed. For the next two hours, Luka cycled between violence, sprinting away, calming down, resting and talking, and then charging himself up again to fight. Eventually he became exhausted. It was around three a.m. when he finally went to bed.

Now back at my house, Luka still wants the vape back from

his dad. We tell him together that we can't let him have it, and his dad leaves. Within a few minutes Luka explodes in anger, starts screaming at me, then runs out the front door.

I follow him to see which way he's going, but by the time I'm out on the street, he is completely out of sight. Philip gets in the car and starts looking for him.

I am panicked. Hearing how aggressive he got with his dad the night before, learning that he is planning on robbing people or businesses in order to get money and that he is worried about being beaten up if he doesn't pay back his debts, and knowing that he's had thoughts of suicide, I am terrified he will hurt himself or someone else.

So I do something I never dreamed I'd do: I call the police.

While waiting for them, I text families in our neighborhood who know Luka and ask them to please let me know if he shows up at their house.

The police arrive, take a report, and leave to start looking for him. Philip is still driving around the neighborhood, and I want to go too, but my younger two kids are sleeping upstairs and I can't leave them alone. Plus someone needs to be home in case Luka returns.

My friend Cat, who got my text about Luka running away, shows up at my door. She's one of the very few people who know the details of the past few years of my life—the worries, the frustrations, the stress. She sits down on the other side of the sofa I'm crouched on. "You don't have to talk if you don't feel like talking, Kristina," she says. "I'll just sit here with you. I don't want you to be alone."

Hours pass and Cat sits with me. She has children and is juggling numerous stressors of her own. But she sits with me. She's not trying to give me advice or cheer me up, which wouldn't work. She's not trying to fix anything. She just quietly sits while I cry. We humans often think we need to do something big in order to help, to give support, to show we care. The wanting to do something big stops us from doing something small. Sometimes the greatest gift we can give someone is to just sit with them.

Eventually, that same night, Luka comes home and goes straight to his room. The police officers return to the house and head upstairs to have a conversation with him. I'm hoping that maybe they can talk some sense into him, at least enough to stop him from running away again. I'm desperate for everything to get better.

But ten days later, everything gets worse.

It's a Tuesday evening, right after Easter weekend. Philip's parents dropped off Easter cards that are now sitting on the kitchen counter. Luka walks into the kitchen and notices that the card with his name on it is open. Then he sees that Ari, his younger brother, has a twenty-dollar bill in his card. Luka assumes (correctly) that he was gifted money as well, but that we took it from the card. These days, when Luka gets cash from someone, I take it and put it in a savings account designated for him. I don't want him to have it because I know he will use it to purchase drugs. Luka takes his brother's cash and puts it in his room. It takes a few hours, but my youngest eventually notices that his card is empty. I go straight into Luka's room, search his dresser, and find not only the money but also more drug paraphernalia. I confiscate all of it. I don't confront Luka this time like I used to.

Within an hour, though, Luka notices what I did and storms into my bedroom screaming. He is more enraged than I have seen before, and he is threatening me. He decides that he's going to run away again. Philip stands against the door, blocking it so that Luka can't leave. We ask Luka to please sit down and take a breath. Let's talk about this. He slams his entire body into Philip, trying to get him to move. He's unsuccessful, which makes him even angrier. "You guys are just gonna send me to fucking rehab, aren't you? Fuck you!" He grabs a large glass of water that is sitting nearby and throws it against the wall where I'm standing. It shatters into pieces all over the carpet. I keep my voice calm. I ask him again to please sit down or lie down on our bed and try to calm down. He charges at Philip again and then spits on him. He looks back at me and screams, "Is that calm enough for you, bitch?"

As much as I don't want to, I feel like outside help is my

only resort. I call the police and ask them to please send someone over. Then I call my mother-in-law, who lives just minutes away. "Judy, I need you to come over right now and pick up Matea and Ari. As quickly as you can." She doesn't ask any questions. She can tell by my tone and Luka's screaming in the background that this is urgent.

Luka is punching at Philip's chest as Philip is pushing him away. At one point, Luka turns to come at me. Worried that he'll hurt me physically, Philip quickly restrains him. Philip graduated from college with a degree in psychology and, thinking he might want to be a therapist someday, he took a job working at a residential center for boys ages six to twelve. While there, he was trained in using therapeutic restraint on a child who is hurting himself or others. The purpose of the restraint is to keep the child safe while they de-escalate. Two years into working at the center, Philip completely changed his career trajectory and eventually became an accountant. Never did he think this extreme training might be something he'd use at home. Not with his stepson, whom he's loved as his own for a decade now. But it's hard to restrain a strong fifteen-year-old. Philip and Luka end up on the floor, Philip still holding him down. Luka can barely move his hands, but he starts grabbing for the broken glass from the carpet, and manages to get a piece. He tries to cut himself and stab Philip. "Get the fuck off me!" he screams.

I quickly kneel down and wrestle the glass out of his hand, then try to move the rest of the glass scattered all over the floor out of his reach. In the midst of this chaos, Ari, who is four years old at the time, knocks on the door. "Mommy. Daddy. I need some water." I don't think he actually needs water. I think he's heard too much and he's scared.

I press my face against the door. I try to make my voice sound as gentle and sweet as possible, but it is shaky and full of urgency. "Ari, I need you to go downstairs with Matea. Right away. Okay? Grammy's coming to get you so that you can have a sleepover at her house."

"Why is it so loud in there, Mommy?"

"Don't worry, buddy. Everything is okay. Just go downstairs and wait for Grammy."

The tears I've been trying so hard to hold back are now pouring out of me. I feel defeated and scared. I can tell that Luka feels defeated and scared too, though his desperation is coming out as rage. I can see in his eyes how much he hates himself and I need him to know he is so loved. Even now. Even in this moment. So I get down to his level. His hand is bloody, and I'm not even sure if it's his blood or Philip's. Despite the chaos, Philip is still calmly trying to get Luka to settle down. I put my face next to Luka's, and look him straight in the eyes. "I love you," I say. Tears are streaming down my face, and he spits at me. I don't move. "I love you." He spits more. "I love you. I love you. I love you."

Luka eventually stops fighting to get out of Philip's arms. Philip lets him go. The three of us are now quietly sitting on the floor. Luka breaks the silence. "When I get out of jail, I will come back here and hurt all of you."

Our standstill here is broken when a few minutes later, we hear the police enter the house. Luka runs out to the balcony. I'm worried he'll try to jump. I hear the officers walking up the stairs and I let them know where we're located, but that I can't open the bedroom door. During Luka and Philip's altercation, the top of the door pushed through the frame and got stuck. The officers ram through the door, enter the bedroom, and take in the broken glass and blood on the carpet. I direct them to the balcony, where Luka is standing and crying. They move to handcuff him, and Luka doesn't resist. One of the officers walks him out of the house, while the other takes photos of the bedroom. Then he takes photos of Philip's bloody arms.

"Let me get down a report and you can press charges."

"What happens if I press charges?" I ask.

"He goes to jail."

"And then what? Is there a psychiatrist who can see him there? Because my kid needs help. My kid needs serious help."

I look at Philip. I can see that he agrees with me.

The officer looks at us with disappointment and disdain. "Sometimes the best way to teach these types of kids a lesson is by showing them what it's like to be locked up for a bit."

I feel pressured. I feel scolded. It's as if the officer is accusing us of spoiling or enabling our child. He sees a bad kid who needs to be punished. I see an ill kid who needs space and support to heal.

I repeat, "My kid needs help."

"Fine. You can change your mind later and still press charges. For now, I guess if you want, we can put him on a 5150. It's a seventy-two-hour psychiatric hold, and he can get assessed by a psychiatrist. But if I were you, seeing the scene I'm looking at right now, I would press charges and show him how the real world works."

As a parent, it's hard to know when to trust your gut and when to override that instinct and make sure it's not fear, pride, or an assumption dressed up as vital intuition. Jail won't help Luka in this situation, the same way my slapping him didn't help. In this moment I choose to trust my instinct. I am very well aware that if we don't get Luka the proper help now, he could someday end up in prison.

Twenty minutes later, I am standing outside of my home, barefoot. Luka sits handcuffed in the back of the cop car. I ask the police officers if I can speak with my son before they take him. They don't seem pleased by this request, but they agree to give me a minute. I walk up to the vehicle expecting them to open the door, but they barely roll down the window. I try to slide my hand through to reach my son, but the opening is too small.

"Officer, please. He's in handcuffs. He can't hurt anyone. Please open the door and let me talk to my son."

My request is denied.

I put my face close to the small opening, trying to hold back the brand-new round of tears ready to burst out of me.

"I love you, Luka. You're going to be okay. You don't have to be scared, all right? We're going to get you help and you're going to be okay."

He looks me straight in the eye and mouths, "I hate you." Then he turns his body away from me.

Part of me knows that I did the right thing by calling the cops and asking them to put him on a psychiatric hold, but part of me just wants to scream, "I changed my mind! I changed my mind! Let him out. I can handle this. I can help him. I'll tuck him into bed the way I did when he was little. He'll get some rest and we'll figure it out. Please open the car door, remove the cuffs, and give my child back to me."

I remember the day he was born. It's hard to describe the feeling you get when your newborn is placed on your chest for the very first time. The sensation takes your breath away in the most heart-filling way. Everything seems surreal and you feel so vulnerable yet so whole.

Watching that cop car drive away with my child in it takes my breath away in the most heartbreaking way. Everything seems surreal and I feel so vulnerable and so empty.

I can't move. I have nowhere to go. I don't have my go-to distraction: tending to my other children.

Philip is on the phone with his dad going over paperwork from the police officers. He's finding numerous ways to stay occupied because doing is easier than feeling in heavy moments like these.

Yet I just stand there. I feel stuck. I don't want to go inside and face the mess. I'm not allowed to follow the cop car to the emergency room. There are no good options. I'm lost.

I don't even remember walking up the stairs, but somehow I make my way back to my bedroom, the room that hours before felt like a scene from a nightmare. I should clean up the bloodstains on the carpet and vacuum the shattered glass, but I can't deal with it all at the moment. It's too much. Everything is too much.

I crawl into bed, eyes wide open, with my phone in my hand, waiting for a call from the emergency room. The only thing more terrifying than the chaos of the past few hours is the silence I now find surrounding me. The only thing scarier than the known, no matter how loud or aggressive, is the quiet of the unknown.

My mind starts racing.

How much of this is my fault? What did I do? What did I not do? Did I get him help soon enough? Is it too late? Did I get him the right kind of help? Did I put too much pressure on him? Did I not give him enough grace? Did I encourage him enough in his interests and strengths?

With each new thought, the self-interrogation gets louder.

Is this because I divorced his dad? Was I too strict? Was I too lenient? Did I do enough to stop him from comparing himself to his sister? What did I overlook? What did I do wrong?

My self-abuse is screaming at me and I don't even attempt to restrain the thoughts rushing in.

After another hour or so of this, I take a deep breath and whisper out loud, "No, thank you."

I've spent my career encouraging other parents to give themselves more credit than criticism and more grace than judgment, and now, as impossible as it seems, I need to take my own advice.

No, thank you. I'm not picking up that baggage. Not tonight. I'm not picking up that judgment. I'm not picking up that guilt.

No, thank you.

And then the tears, which took a break for a few minutes, return.

Who is going to check on him in the middle of the night like I've been doing every night for the past year?

After I found out that Luka was struggling with suicidal thoughts, I returned to the routine that had comforted me when he was a newborn: checking on him multiple times a night, bringing my face close to his as he slept to make sure he was still breathing.

Parents often think we have more control than we do—as if my checking on him had any power to keep my son alive. The story I kept telling myself, the lie about how much power I have, caused so much self-abuse. If you think you actually have the power to control something, then when things don't turn out well, it's all your fault.

No, thank you.

Morning arrives and I am still lying wide awake, cell phone in hand. The lock screen on my phone for the past few years has been one simple sentence: "This isn't about me." I created it as a reminder, once my career took off, to not get sucked into all the hype, to stay humble and focused on the reason I started making videos in the first place: to help others feel less alone.

But now, suddenly, after staring at that phone screen all night to make sure I didn't miss a call, that sentence takes on a whole new meaning. This isn't about me. This isn't the time to think about all the things I could have, should have done.

This isn't the time to treat myself like some sort of victim in this situation—poor Kristina had to call the cops on her struggling son. This isn't about me. This is about my child. And though I need to be gentle with myself right now, there's a big difference between self-care and self-pity. I remind myself that—just as I've always said the only thing harder than raising a teenager is being a teenager—the only thing heavier than parenting a child with mental illness is being a child with mental illness.

Around ten a.m., the phone finally buzzes. A nurse tells me that they're still waiting on a bed in a psychiatric hospital to open up, but I am allowed to visit Luka in the emergency room. The nurse warns me that we will have no privacy. Patients who are put on a psychiatric hold are kept in beds in the ER hallway so that they can constantly be monitored to ensure their safety.

I arrive at the hospital and am given a visitor sticker. As the security guard opens the double doors from the waiting room into the emergency room, I see my son at the end of the long hallway. I am about halfway down the hall when he notices me. He puts his arm out and points his finger at me. "Get the hell out!"

His words stop me in my tracks. This isn't personal, I try to remind myself. But I'm struggling to fully believe it in the moment.

I keep walking toward him, trying desperately to ease the fear and sadness and anxiety brewing inside me.

I say calmly and quietly, "Hi, Luka. Did you get any sleep?" He won't look at me.

I notice that he has no socks or shoes, and suddenly remember that he was placed in the cop car barefoot. He's wearing shorts and a thin T-shirt. "Do you want me to ask for another blanket? Are you cold?"

"I'm serious! Get out. Leave! Now!"

I'm not sure what to do. I have been up all night with no answers, worried sick about him, wondering if he's scared, waiting for the moment I'd finally get to see him, and now he doesn't want me here? I'm feeling frustrated and selfish and I have no idea what the correct move is for a parent. Do I ignore his demand and stay? Do I simply walk out of here and leave him? Is he just testing me, the way kids sometimes do, like when you push against the lap bar on a roller coaster to make sure it's steady and safe? Is he testing me to make sure I'm a steady and safe place for him, that I won't let him drop? Or does he really want me gone?

I see his rage, and I want to respect his space. I realize that forcing my presence on him right now won't be constructive. But do I really just leave? It's a delicate dance, letting him lead and yet knowing he needs me to guide him. The problem is, I don't feel equipped for the job of a guide right now.

I do the best I can given the circumstances, even though my best right now feels pretty mediocre.

"I love you so much, Luka. I'll leave, but I'll come back."

Forty minutes later, I am back with socks, shoes, his favorite sweatshirt, and his favorite smoothie.

"I didn't know if you had anything to eat yet. So, I wanted to bring you—"

"I don't want you here. Just fucking leave!" He still won't look at me. He still hates me.

Everything inside me wants to justify my good intentions. I just want him to know that I'm coming from a place of love, not anger, punishment, or resentment. I'm trying desperately to help him, and his therapist even suggested I call the cops if things got out of hand. But I know my reasons are not what my son needs right now. So instead I simply say, "I'll come back a little later. I'll bring you lunch."

I head straight to his favorite burger joint and sit in the parking lot for over an hour. There's not a single place on this earth that feels like the right place to be except next to him, but I'm not wanted there.

I return to the ER again, this time knowing exactly what I'm walking into. I make my way down the long hall, and I'm startled by a familiar face. I have inadvertently made eye contact with a man from our neighborhood. He works at the hospital. I don't know him well, but his kids go to the same school as mine.

His wife knows who I am and follows my social media pages. I say nothing and keep walking. Paranoid thoughts (aka normal, human thoughts) start rushing in. *Did he hear my child scream at me earlier? Was he here last night when the cops brought him in? He must be aware that my child is on a psychiatric hold because his bed is in the hallway. If he tells his wife any of this, who will she tell and how fast will this spread?*

Deep breath. No, thank you. No, thank you. No, thank you.

I make it to Luka's bed and start removing the burger and fries and extra BBQ sauce, which he loves, from the paper bag. I try to sit on the chair next to his bed.

"No! Get out!"

"Okay. I love you. I'll come back."

I return again two hours later. I can see that he has eaten his burger. But before I can speak, he says, "You're wasting your fucking time. Stop coming to see me."

The calm I was able to muster earlier leaves me. My eyes fill with tears; my voice is strong but shaky as I say, "Now, you listen to me. You will *never* be a waste of my time, and I will *never* stop showing up for you."

I slowly sit on the chair next to him. This time he lets me. "I don't want you to talk," he says. I nod.

I know what it's like to be in your darkest moments, confused and terrified, while the people you need the most don't show up for you. You start to feel unlovable. And I know that as much as my son seems to hate me right now, he hates himself more.

After some time, Luka breaks the silence. "Just so you know, when I get the hell out of here, I'm going to change my name, and you will never see me again."

I break his no-speaking rule. "Luka, when you get out of here, you're going to get better, and then you're going to use the hell you've been through to help someone else walk through theirs."

And for the first time since he turned away from me while sitting in the back of the cop car, he looks me straight in the eye. He says nothing, but he looks at me. And I can tell by his look that he really wants to believe me.

A few hours later we are told that a bed has opened up in a psychiatric hospital an hour away. I ask the medics if I can drive him there. I'm told no.

"Can I at least ride in the ambulance with him?"

"No."

Two men bring over a gurney and Luka gets on. One of the medics says to him, "If you have any sort of itch, scratch it now because it's going to be an hour drive and you won't be able to use your hands." And with that, they begin to strap down his wrists and ankles.

"No, no, please, that's not necessary. Please don't do that to him. He's calm. Don't do this to him."

"I'm sorry, ma'am. This is protocol. It's for his own safety. We can't take any risks when he's in the back of the ambulance."

Once they finish completely strapping him down, he turns his head toward me and stares at me with pure disgust. It's as if he's saying to me, "Mom, what did I do to get you to hate me this much?"

He's completely helpless and terrified, and I can't make him feel safe or loved—the most basic, absolute minimum things a mother should be able to give her child.

And then they take him away. I stand there, in the middle of the emergency room, and I can't move. Everything around me seems to be continuing as usual, but I can't move.

Lie #4

Progress Is a
Straight Line

———⊙———

It's dark because you are trying too hard.

Lightly child, lightly. Learn to do everything lightly.

Yes, feel lightly even though you're feeling deeply.

Just lightly let things happen and lightly cope with
them. . . .

So throw away your baggage and go forward.

There are quicksands all about you, sucking at your feet,

trying to suck you down into fear and self-pity and despair.

That's why you must walk so lightly. Lightly my darling . . .

—ALDOUS LEONARD HUXLEY

———⊙———

I t's weird how the world just keeps spinning. There are still groceries to buy, dirty laundry to wash, dogs that need walking, work projects to complete.

And a child to convince that life is worth living.

The day after Luka is transferred to the hospital, I am on a call with the psychiatrist assigned to him. After a long interview with me, she tells me that Luka has been cooperative, answering all her questions as she tries to dig in and figure out the root of his depression and the best steps forward. She tells me she's adjusting his medication and is hopeful it will make a difference. She then transfers me to a staff member who will go over all the visitation guidelines. There are limited and specific times I'm allowed to call Luka. Visiting hours are restricted to one hour each day. To protect the privacy of patients, visitors are required to leave all personal belongings, including cell phones, in the car. All items brought to the patients must be screened by staff. Any item that could be used to harm oneself is not allowed, including clothing with strings, ties, laces, or underwire. No entering patients' rooms, including your child's room. All visits are supervised by staff.

Before being transferred to the hospital, Luka made it very clear to me that he did not want any visitors. I choose to show up anyway. It's the only thing I know to do. In the past, whenever a parenting challenge made me feel helpless or nervous or flat-out stupid, showing up felt like the only thing I could offer. And time and again, showing up has been valuable.

I am determined to be there for Luka every single day.

But on that first day, I don't show up for the visit. I end up missing the slot because of an accident on the highway that backs up traffic for miles. I am devastated and frantic, but there isn't anything I can do. I add yet another guilt badge to my motherhood vest.

On the second day, I make it on time. I'm nervous. Luka is cold with me. I talk to him quietly. There is no privacy. I sit in a hallway with other parents and their children. Some seem to hate their parents. Some are snuggling up to their family members. Some are sitting alone, hoping for a visitor who never comes.

After I leave, I don't remove the visitor wristband. I sleep with it on. It makes me feel closer to him.

During my third visit, Luka sits with me and talks. Nothing deep. He just fills me in on his daily schedule. He tells me he's been painting and writing some poetry. He doesn't want to share it, though. As I'm leaving, two girls get into a physical fight. The staff runs over to separate them. The scene frightens me. But Luka doesn't seem fazed. I worry that a place like this could add more trauma to his plate. I worry that seeing things like this could normalize stress that I can't conceive of as being normal.

The seventy-two-hour psychiatric hold ends up being a ten-day hold.

On my fourth visit, Luka shows me one of his paintings. He's warming up to me. He tells me the support groups have been helpful. And he's learning breathing techniques that are helping him keep calm. When the visiting hour is over, he unexpectedly wraps his arms around me tightly, the way he used to when he was little and would run into me for an embrace, almost knocking me over. My body tenses for a split second and then melts into his arms. After months of no affection from him, in the cold hospital hallway, he's giving me the kind of hug in which my feet leave the ground for a few seconds.

"Thank you, Mom," he says, his arms still around me. "You did the right thing."

I cry for hours after that visit.

My boy is back.

The visits mostly go well, but my hope for progress is crushed when I find out that Luka has figured out how to get Benadryl and is snorting it to get high. He noticed that some kids were getting Benadryl for their allergies, and he managed to convince them to "cheek" it for him—to pretend to swallow the pills, but hide them between the gum and the cheek instead. Once the staff catches on, they become much stricter and more thorough about checking the inside of every patient's mouth after administering medication.

It's a frustrating setback, and another reminder not to let my hopes get too high. Except I don't know how to navigate this process without hope.

Despite the Benadryl incident, Luka's attitude and openness in groups continue to improve and grow. But he also needs more intervention and more time for doctors to monitor his reaction to the medication changes. The staff recommends he be transferred to a residential treatment center. Our insurance will cover most of his stay.

I'm relieved when I am given permission to drive him there myself.

Being outside with Luka again feels strange. We're beyond the confinement of those hospital walls, with no one watching over us. We get in the car, and Luka immediately asks if he can pick the music. He didn't have access to music while in the hospital and he misses it. Before he cranks the volume all the way up, he turns to me and tells me he wants to stop drinking and using drugs. He's going to work hard at it. I tell him I believe in him. The entire ninety-minute drive, music I absolutely hate is blasting way too loud, and for the first time ever, I don't mind at all. Luka is singing and smiling, drumming on his knees, and he looks so alive. I keep glancing at him and the same thought repeats over and over in my head.

My boy is back.

We arrive at the residential center, which is really just a house that looks like any other house. We are greeted by a staff member and a therapist. They have stacks of paperwork for me to fill out, but I need to first say goodbye to Luka so that they can show him to his room and help him through orientation. Luka and I face each other and my eyes immediately well up with tears. Before I can say a word, he puts his arms around me. "Don't worry, Mom. This is good. This will be good for me. I'm going to get better here."

My boy is back.

Visits are now only once a week. Each visit starts with a support group. The first half is just for the parents, then the boys join us for the second half. After that we have free time when we can play board games and eat lunch together at the house. I spend Mother's Day visiting Luka. Instead of being spoiled with a typical Mother's Day brunch at a nice restaurant with French toast and mimosas, I'm sitting next to Luka in a support group. And there is no place I'd rather be. Later in the visit, Luka opens his notebook to show me what he wrote in his journal that morning.

> *My mom is always there for me, even when I'm acting my worst. She is my biggest cheerleader and gives me the best advice. I love my mom more than anyone because we have a special bond. Back when we were poor, my mom worked three separate jobs and made sure we had a bunkbed while she slept on the ground. She makes me the most incredible birthday cakes. She is caring and compassionate.*

My boy is back.

A few days later, Luka calls me, but instead of updating me on his day like he usually does, he is sobbing. "I can't do it, Mom. I can't live anymore. I don't want to."

"Luka. What happened? I know you were having days where you felt your depression strongly, but even on those days, you seemed to be doing better."

"Nothing happened. I just can't do this anymore. I don't want to live. I don't think I can ever feel okay. I don't think I will ever feel truly happy."

I am allowed only a ten-minute call. I don't know how to

have this conversation in ten minutes. I'm panicking inside, but I calmly say to him, "Remember when I drove you from the psychiatric hospital to the residential treatment center? We had the view of the ocean on one of those perfect California spring days. You blasted your music and opened the sunroof of my car. I looked over at you and you were smiling. You sang at the top of your lungs. You felt so alive. You felt content. Listen to me. You can feel that again! I need you to believe you can. If you've felt joy before, you can feel it again. You *will* feel it again."

"I don't think I will."

Setback. I feel my chest tighten with fear.

We've been climbing this mountain together, but the trail is turning to slippery sand. Is Luka sliding away from me again?

In the following week, Luka is either sad or angry during our calls. He's feeling hopeless and no longer optimistic about healing. He tells me being there is a waste of time and he just wants to come home. A few more days pass, and Luka is still feeling down. Then I get a call from one of the therapists at the center. I am told Luka destroyed all the upstairs motion sensors. He violently pulled them out of the walls and damaged some other property. He has made threats to continue destroying property and is encouraging his peers to join him in distracting others from the center's programming and support groups. He has been removed from the general group and is allowed only to meet one-on-one with staff, until he can show that he is able to move forward in a positive manner. If things escalate, the staff might have to get the police involved.

Setback.

During our next visit, Luka pleads with his dad and me to take him home. When we tell him we can't yet, he storms upstairs where the bedrooms are located, and we can hear the sound of furniture being thrown around. The staff asks us to leave immediately so they can de-escalate the situation.

Setback.

The emotional seesaw I'm suddenly attempting to balance feels like some cruel game the universe is playing with me. He was better. I witnessed it. I got my hopes up. And now this.

I schedule a call with the psychiatrist at the center. The tone of my voice is desperate as I plead with him to quickly make some changes. "Something is off. He was doing better and now he's getting much worse. The new medication that was added isn't working. Please help him."

At this point, Luka has tried five different medications since first seeing a psychiatrist. He is currently on three. The one that seemed to be helping him the most at the hospital came with a side effect of almost nonstop shaking. It was hard for him to even sleep. The doctor at the residential center took him off that medication and replaced it with a similar one. The shaking stopped. But did the depression get worse?

Within two weeks, to my complete relief, Luka starts to settle down. The angry outbursts subside. I'm not sure if the new coping skills he's learning in therapy are working their magic, if the withdrawal from drugs has dissipated, or if we've found the right prescription medication combination to support his healing. I'm just relieved.

In one of the support groups, a mother shares that this is the third residential treatment center for her son. Another parent chimes in, "For our son too."

Third? *Third?* My chest tightens. My hands get clammy. Why didn't the first time work? How bad did things have to get at home after residential treatment to lead those boys back? I thought these programs were supposed to work. We can't do this again. That can't be our story.

Luka and I have been making great strides in our weekly joint therapy sessions, and the progress feels really good. In one of our last sessions at the center, he tells me that he misses how close we used to be. He wants that relationship again and he's sorry for all the pain he's caused me. I'm almost vibrating with joy—we're about to finally break through to the next level of his healing and leave this chapter behind. Luka takes a deep breath and continues, "I know we can't be close if I'm lying. I don't want to do that anymore. I want to build trust with you."

I love hearing this. This is the Luka I've missed so much.

He used to be so brutally honest with me when he was younger, even about things he worried he would get in trouble for.

My boy is back.

But then he looks at me and says, "I know you might not understand, but since I don't want to hide things and I want to be honest with you, I want you to know that as soon as I leave residential, I'm going to start using again."

Major setback. I start to feel dizzy. Luka is making yet another U-turn, and I just don't think I have the stomach to course-correct us.

No. This is not where this conversation is supposed to go.

I take a deep breath now. "Luka." I pause and remind myself to stay very calm. No panic. No stress in my tone. Calm.

"Luka, I appreciate your honesty. I want to acknowledge that, because it's a huge step in a positive direction. And you're right, we can't have a close relationship without trust. However, I am not going to approve of you doing drugs and I am not going to allow any drugs in my home. I will do what I have to do to help you stop. I just need you to want to stop."

Luka and I go back and forth for a little while, both staying calm during our discussion. The therapist is chiming in every once in a while to help us communicate more clearly with each other, and to help Luka understand my point of view. Realizing that he's not going to convince me, Luka stops talking and puts his head down. He looks defeated. I notice tears dripping onto his jeans. I keep talking but I can tell he's no longer hearing me. After a few minutes, he looks up, still crying. "Mom, if the only thing keeping you from killing yourself was being high, would you do drugs?"

We're holding eye contact and I can see the pain in his face. It's as if he's begging me to rescue him from the hell he's trapped in. I wish I could. I wish I could take it all away, switch places with him, do anything just to help him feel okay, feel healthy, feel some hope. And for the first time, I understand on a much deeper level that he is genuinely convinced that his only options are to live high and numb or die sober. I see the fear in his eyes. He doesn't want to end things, but he is scared of what he might do if he has to continue to feel his depression.

I scoot closer to him on the sofa and put my hands on his. He's being honest, and I will too.

"Yes, Luka. If I thought the only thing that could keep me from killing myself was being high, I would do drugs. But I have to believe. . . . I *have* to believe that there is a better way. And I need you to not give up yet on trying to find a better way."

"Mom, I've tried so many other things. Look where I'm at right now, in a program with all this support, and I still just want to die."

Setback.

The day after Luka is released from the residential program, we are scheduled to fly to Croatia to visit my family. I'm
scared to bring him back to our house for that one night before
the trip, so I stay with him in a hotel near the airport. Taking
advice from counselors and doctors, I have changed every aspect of his bedroom at home in order to eliminate any triggers
from the place where he self-medicated and so often contemplated suicide, but I'm still nervous to bring him back there.
Plus, I don't want him trying to contact people who might be
able to get him drugs. He has expressed his certainty that he
will be able to use drugs "responsibly." And he reminds me of
this intention every time he sees concern in my eyes.

Before our trip, I email my parents, sisters, and brother-in-
law, asking them to get rid of or lock up any alcohol or pills
they might have in their homes. They oblige.

Luka normally loves being in Croatia, but this time it's obvious he's really depressed. Most days he's calm, but he has a
few angry outbursts. One day, he repeatedly punches a wall
until his hands bleed. I know now that the physical pain dis-
tracts him from the pain of depression. Another day, he hides
under a bed for a few hours, just to get away from everyone
and everything.

Setback.

We return from Croatia and even though he has only two

years of high school left, we mutually decide to move him to a new school. Just like with his made-over room, I don't want him going back to the environment where he had so many dark thoughts. The new school is much smaller and has a great reputation for prioritizing mental health.

The very first day at his new school, Luka gets high.

Setback.

I can't tolerate more chaos. I feel like I'm drowning.

Just a few days later, Luka tells me he wants to drop out and never go back. Not to this school. Not to any school. He hates it. He hates everything.

"It's fucking stupid and there's no point to it! Any of it!"

He's angry and pacing. And then suddenly there's a shift. His pacing slows. His rage morphs from thunderous to somber.

"What is it, Luka? I know you hate school in general, but the teachers at this school seem so encouraging and I haven't heard you complain about any of your classes. Help me understand." He remains silent for another moment, and then he tells me that there's a girl at this school who is targeting him. She approaches him almost every day and says, "No one wants you here."

When she sees kids talking to him during recess or lunch, she waits until he's alone and then walks up to him and quietly says, "If you only knew what they say behind your back."

It's so hard trying to fit in when you're surrounded by students who already have a history with each other and established friendships, especially when you're struggling with depression. The last thing he needs is someone taunting him.

I am enraged and launch into problem-solving mode. I try to convince Luka that we should meet with the staff and tell them about this girl. He is extremely resistant, but eventually he gives in.

The meeting goes well. The teachers and administrators are compassionate and determined to make sure the bullying stops. They don't seem surprised that this particular girl would target Luka this way. But the meeting doesn't bring Luka relief. He's nervous that calling her out will lead to retaliation from her and her friends.

Things have returned to the way they were before he was hospitalized: Luka is angry, isolating, using drugs, and confronting suicidal thoughts.

Setback. Setback. Setback.

I am told over and over again that setbacks are a normal part of healing. Sure, I get it. But when I think of a setback, I think two steps forward, one step back. That's a setback. This feels like two steps forward, ninety steps back. These are not setbacks. This is speeding in reverse with failed brakes.

I can't do this. I am completely out of ideas.

Luka has been hospitalized. He's had three different psychiatrists trying to adjust and supervise his medication. He's been in individual therapy and group therapy and family therapy. He's had full-time support at a residential center, talking through all his emotions, learning coping skills and breathwork and meditation, working on anger management and expressing his needs in a healthy way, being encouraged in his strengths and talents. He's participated in support groups with his peers. He has been loved and encouraged and cared for and prayed for.

How is he not in a better place?

If all these professionals haven't had the power to help him heal, what power do I alone have? And have I even done enough? And how much is enough?

What I desperately need right now is a story with a beginning, a middle, and a happy ending. I want the movie version of this ordeal. Luka deserves to get better because that's what's supposed to happen. I want the version where he went through a really hard time, he struggled, we hit some terrifying moments, but then things started to fall into place, and now we get to experience a resolution. Healing wins. Credits roll.

Every good moment is shadowed by a dark cloud waiting to dump its contents on us. There doesn't seem to be a beginning, middle, and end. There seems to be only grappling for a foothold, and then waiting for the foothold to crumble. I swing between my determination to fix and my fear as each new plan collapses. I want my hope back and I want my son back.

I'm angry. I'm not angry at Luka or the doctors or the therapists. Maybe I'm angry at depression. Maybe I'm angry at myself for not knowing all the things I don't know. Maybe I'm angry that every time my phone rings with an unknown number, I panic that something has happened to my son. Maybe I'm angry that I don't know how to live a life in which I constantly worry about my child killing himself. Maybe I'm angry at uncertainty.

When does it get easier? When does it start to make sense?

And then, out of the blue, Luka has a good day. Nothing remarkable. Just a good day. He gets out of bed in the morning. He brushes his teeth. He doesn't get harassed at school. He turns in his homework. I get a message from his Spanish teacher telling me that Luka was really helpful to another student during class. A good day.

Maybe we're supposed to go through hell days to appreciate that average days are actually amazing days.

My boy is back. Though maybe just for a day. Sometimes just for hours.

During the good moments, I struggle to stay present. My mind tries to fast-forward to the next worry, but my heart so desperately needs to stay right here, in what is true in this very moment, in what is good now.

LIE #4: PROGRESS IS A STRAIGHT LINE

One morning, I wake up to an email from a stranger who stayed up late watching some of my videos.

Thank you for being so real and raw about your past struggles. Your story and your trials have helped me realize that I don't need to be perfect or have all the answers in order to be the parent my children need, and that I too can make it through the impossible days.

I read the message again. And again. Impossible days. I'm not new to impossible days. I'm not new to uncertainty. I'm grateful for this reminder from a stranger.

I'm in such a hopeless place that the only outcomes I keep imagining are bad ones. I'm intelligent enough and have spent enough time in therapy to know that pessimism isn't going to cut it. For my sanity and the sanity of my family, my mindset needs to shift to "Even if bad things happen, I will manage."

I think back on all the awful things that have happened in my life and point out to myself that I somehow got through each one. Those are facts. Those are not just hopes.

I create a post for my followers on social media. "For whoever needs to hear this, next time you feel lost or inadequate, think about all the unmanageable stuff life threw your way.

And yet you managed. You managed the unmanageable. You turned the difficult into doable. You are amazing."

The "whoever" I'm writing to is me.

I have to believe that all the effort put into Luka's health so far has not been in vain. But I also can't live solely for the resolution. My sanity cannot be tied to the progress he is or isn't making. My value can't be attached to any specific results. Because the outcome is beyond my control. And as terrifying as that is, there's a level of acceptance that has to take place in order for me to avoid more tension in an already stressful situation. I struggle to sit with uncertainty.

I remember the hot August day I was in labor with Luka. After hours and hours of contractions, it was time to push, but my body felt so drained and weak and I was scared. "I can't do this," I whispered through tears. "I really don't think I can. I can't do this."

My midwife looked me in the eyes and said, "But you're already doing it. You are already doing it." Ten minutes later, I got to meet Luka.

I know there will be many more days of feeling like I can't. I can't handle any more bad news. I can't watch my son suffer. I can't deal with the fact that I don't know how to help him. I can't carry yet another load of fresh, new stress. I can't manage more sleepless, fear-filled nights. I can't do this.

But I'm already doing it. I'm already doing it.

Lie #5

Good Parents
Are Selfless

———⊙———

I once paid a babysitter to come watch my kids for an hour so I could nap. She showed up, I handed her the money, and I told her I'd be upstairs sleeping with earplugs in. My youngest was a baby, the older two wouldn't stop bickering with each other, my husband was at work, and I was an exhausted hot mess (not that kind of hot). Never have I felt more grateful for some extra cash to spend.

Someone told me it was a waste of money. I quickly countered that it was an investment—an investment in my sanity. Best twenty bucks I've ever spent.

A few years later, after a speaking event, I met a mom who obviously needed a nap. I handed her a twenty-dollar bill and instructions for how to use it.

———⊙———

My fortieth birthday celebration has been in the works for months. The plan is as follows:

On Friday (my actual birthday), my husband is throwing a party for me in the private room of a beautiful restaurant that boasts gorgeous views of Los Angeles. Our closest friends and family will attend. Philip has hired a DJ, rented a photo booth, ordered a cake, and picked out a great menu. From Saturday through Monday, I'll head out on a road trip to Santa Barbara with three of my closest friends. The itinerary for the girls' trip is: fun, relaxation, more fun.

But life doesn't happen in a vacuum, where we can focus on just one plotline. Real life is messy and doesn't unfold one element at a time.

Despite the plan, the days leading up to my birthday were anything but celebratory.

The Tuesday before my birthday was the evening I called the cops on Luka and they took him to the emergency room.

The Wednesday before my birthday, I visited Luka in the ER and then he was transferred to a psychiatric hospital.

The Thursday before my birthday, I was allowed to visit Luka at the hospital for the first time.

Before my life got turned upside down, I was really excited about turning forty and starting this new decade. I love birthdays. I always have. I love them so much that when Luka turned six months old, I decided we should start a tradition in which we celebrate half birthdays. I made him half a cake, sang half of the Happy Birthday song (every other syllable, because complicating things is one of my spiritual gifts), and committed to continuing that tradition with all my kids, every year. And we have.

But now I feel like I'm floating in a dark sea with no energy left to paddle and no land in sight. I tell Philip we need to cancel everything—the party, my girls' trip. This isn't the time. I'm not in the mood, and most important, any kind of celebration feels wrong right now.

I can see the wheels turning in Philip's mind as he takes this in. He pauses and gives me a quick hug before speaking.

"We can do whatever you want. But I don't think you should cancel."

I still can't think straight. So I call my mother-in-law for her advice. She asks, "If you cancel the party, what will you do instead during that time?"

I don't really need to answer, as we both know I'll most likely spend that time lying in my bed, worrying and crying.

She waits a beat and then continues, "I'm not going to tell you what the right thing for you is. Only you can decide that. But maybe being surrounded by people who love you, who genuinely care about you and want to celebrate your life, maybe that would be a good way to spend those hours."

Her words are like the warm embrace I desperately need, and yet accepting her support is uncomfortable because I don't feel worthy of that kind of love right now.

"What do I do?" I ask Philip again. "This feels wrong. I can't have a party when Luka is—"

"Luka is in a safe place. He's probably in the safest place he's been since he started struggling. He's with people who are trained to help him. He can't run away. He can't hurt himself. He's safe. And you deserve a break. I really think you should take this time to do something for you."

Take time to do something for me. I have spent so many years telling mothers, in every way I can reach them, "Do not ever feel guilty taking care of the most important person in your child's life—you!" And yet in this moment when fear and pain and stress and uncertainty have collided to completely cloud my vision, I'm struggling to follow that advice myself.

Do something for me. A night of solid sleep, a good meal, coffee with a friend, a bath . . . those sound like doable options. But a party? A party just days after I have put my son in a psychiatric hospital against his will?

Philip and his mom gently convince me to go through with the entire weekend and I reluctantly agree.

At the party I feel surrounded by love, but also full of sadness and guilt. I can barely touch my food. I am trying to hold it together. I keep wishing Luka were here. He was supposed to be here, sitting right next to me.

I find myself forcing smiles and forcing small talk. Even though all of our guests know Luka has been struggling, and some even know exactly why he isn't present, I feel a stupid responsibility to make sure that the party is fun and not sad. I feel pressure to make sure everyone is having a good time, and not feeling bad for my son or our family. And it all adds to the exhaustion I'm already drowning in. Yet the only person putting that pressure on me is me.

Throughout the evening, judgmental thoughts creep in.

I should be doing something else right now.

I should be researching the best ways to help Luka.

I should be reading a book on mental health.

I should be compiling questions for the doctors and therapists at the hospital.

I should be figuring out the best plan for after he is released.

I should be doing more.

I should be a better mother.

This isn't the first time in my life that I have mistaken constant doing for a sign of a loving, caring human.

As the night goes on, a friend pulls me onto the dance floor, and I completely let loose. I dance and dance until I have blisters on the soles of my feet and sweat dripping down my back. The memories of the past few days that have been playing on a loop in my mind snap off. It's as if my body is desperately trying to release all the emotional toxins it's collected over the past few years. And it feels really good. *Really* good. And right after it feels really good, it feels really bad.

What type of mom dances while her son is in the hospital wanting to die?

The following morning, my friends and I head out for our girls' weekend. The hospital where Luka is staying is located between our house and Santa Barbara. I refuse to miss any visits with him, and the hospital has strict and limited visitation hours, so each day we're away, I'm going to drive there to see him. I let my friends know that I'll be gone for three hours. One hour to drive there. One hour with him. One hour to drive back.

On our first day, my friend Jo beats me to the driver's seat and jumps in, and my friends Cat and Amy hop in the back. "We're going with you. You're not driving there alone."

All three days of our girls' weekend, my friends accompany me on the drive to see Luka. Not because they think I can't handle it, but because they are pure love. Instead of taking advantage of the gorgeous hotel we're staying at, lounging by the pool or shopping or exploring the beautiful scenery of Santa Barbara, they drive me to the hospital, drop me off, then wait for me while I'm with my son. Pure love.

After each visit, I return to that car and immediately fall apart, releasing the tears I held back while visiting Luka. I cry and worry and vent and hope. They listen. They encourage me. And then they gently help me navigate my way back to laughter and joy.

When Luka is transferred to the residential treatment center, I find myself driving from the intake appointment straight to my friend Zach Anner's apartment. I didn't plan this detour, but with the pain I'm weathering, I really need a friendly distraction. From the moment I met Zach, I have felt a special bond with him. He is more like family than just a friend. No matter what life throws my way, he genuinely cares and attentively listens. He is always able to provide a perspective and insight that I might not have considered. And without a doubt, even on the darkest days, regardless of what he or I is struggling through, he makes me laugh harder than anyone else.

Decompressing with him after my weekly visits with Luka becomes a vital routine. We always order Thai food. Our meal is always followed by a second meal of snacks from the produce drawer in his fridge, which has zero produce in it because it is solely dedicated to candy. Reason No. 752 that Zach is a genius.

Over cold Andes mints and KitKats, we chat about our week. Some visits I don't want to talk about Luka and instead need space from my worries. Other visits I unload completely. One day, I admit to Zach that I still feel really crappy and guilty for having that birthday party and the girls' trip mere days after Luka was hospitalized. It all feels so self-centered.

Zach's reaction surprises me: "Don't feel bad. You did him a favor."

"What? What do you mean, I did him a favor?"

"You gave him one less thing to carry."

Zach gets a certain look in his eyes when he's telling me something he really wants me to take in, and so now I lean in, truly listening. "Luka knows how much you love birthdays.

He knew your party was planned for months. Back when I was in high school and really struggling with depression, I put my mom through a lot. I was awful to her at times. So if in addition to that, she had canceled her birthday party because of me, I would still carry that guilt today, two decades later. You saved Luka from yet another thing to feel bad about, yet another thing to feel he destroyed. Going through with the party and that weekend away was actually a gift to Luka."

I sit there in stunned silence, overcome by emotion, processing what he has just said. I feel my shoulders relax. All these weeks of carrying that unnecessary guilt for celebrating at the "wrong" time, feeling like a terrible, selfish person—all that self-judgment vanishes with his words.

Somewhere along the way, I got tricked into believing that if my loved ones are suffering, I need to suffer as well, as if only my suffering could express the empathy and concern I feel.

During hard times, I find myself dogged by the idea that I can enjoy life only when the turbulent season has passed and life calms down. Once Luka is happy, then I'll be happy. Once Luka is healthy, then I can start feeling healthy. Once Luka feels peace, then I can feel peace. Once Luka is able to fully live his life, then I will fully live mine.

Zach's words help me see that that's a hell of a lot of pressure to put on someone.

What if my child is never completely healthy?

Positive emotions shouldn't be a reward I try to earn, especially when so often "earning" that reward is contingent on circumstances completely beyond my control. Life will be hard more often than it will be easy. I can't keep waiting on the sidelines until it stops being painful before I choose to actually get in the game and play. Depriving myself of fully living and instead immersing myself in suffering 24-7 isn't going to help Luka. His struggles are a big, vital part of my story. But they are not my whole story.

I am giving myself permission to feel more than one emotion at a time. Pain and joy can coexist. I know this. I've felt it. And I'm done feeling guilty about it. Caring for someone else doesn't have to mean abandoning caring for myself.

Throughout my childhood, I watched my grandmother prepare meals for family and guests, spending hours in the kitchen cooking, then serving it all, getting up from the table every few minutes to make sure everyone had everything they needed, and finally cleaning up—rarely sitting down long enough to fully enjoy all her hard work. And everyone called her generous and kind and selfless.

The word *selfless* is defined as being concerned more with the needs and wishes of others than with one's own, or having no concern for self.

How did this become okay, and even praised? How is a parent supposed to keep their sanity if they have no concern for self?

We applaud people for putting others' needs above their own. Why can't I care about my son's needs and my needs with equal passion? Why does one have to take precedence over the other? Does everything in the world have to be a comparison, a competition? It's obvious I'm capable of caring deeply for more than one human. I have three children. I care for all of them equally. But somehow if I care about myself as much as I care about my children, it's looked down upon.

I spent years putting myself on the back burner, people-pleasing, making sure everyone else was okay and had what they needed without pausing to ask myself if I was okay and had what I needed. I don't want to live like that anymore, especially now, when I am exhausted and worried and heartbroken. I want to be as generous and helpful and loving to myself as I am to anyone else.

If I am being completely honest, I also couldn't fully detach from the feedback and criticism of other people. If someone who knows that my son is hospitalized sees me laughing or dancing, will they think I don't care about my child and label me insensitive? Once I start entertaining the comments of others, and worrying about protecting myself and my family from their impact, I find myself explaining and excusing and justifying my behavior. Like I should always be wearing a T-shirt that reads: I

CARE THAT MY CHILD IS SICK AND I'M ALSO DESPERATE FOR SOME
LEVITY AND CONNECTION AND JOY. Or, PLEASE LET ME BE HAPPY
FOR A FEW HOURS. MY BODY NEEDS A BREAK FROM CRYING AND
PANICKING!

The moments in my life when I've genuinely nailed the "I
don't care what anyone thinks" attitude have been the healthiest and most productive for me. Other people's judgments, or
even my completely unjustified fears of other people's judgments, hobble me and keep my healing journey stuck in slow
motion.

Life is messy. It keeps moving forward. It doesn't pause because my son is clinically depressed. Even when our most important people are struggling, the bills still come due. During
the time Luka is in the hospital and the residential center, I
have work commitments that I can't just shelve. There are
deadlines for my first book, contracts with sponsors whom I
owe videos, tour dates for shows. It's not lost on me that all
my work is geared toward encouraging parents, making them
laugh and helping them feel less alone—and yet I've never felt
more isolated.

The morning after I drive Luka to the residential center,
I'm scheduled to do a photo shoot for my book cover. The
shoot has been on the calendar for months, and many people's
schedules depend on me following through. When I first
added this date to my calendar, it was with a flutter of excite-

ment. My first book, my first cover! But now I'm in the middle of a heartbreak. I can't recapture the thrill.

But I head to the studio as planned, sit down in the makeup chair, and ask the makeup artist if she can work her magic to make me look rested and less puffy. As I sit there, watching myself in the mirror, my mind races with the long to-do list of logistics that need to be taken care of: call the insurance company, get a copy of Luka's school transcript, sign him up for an independent study so that he can finish at least one class at the center and not fall too far behind, schedule the first family therapy session with Luka's new counselor, schedule a meeting with his new psychiatrist, move my schedule around so I don't miss any weekly visits at the center . . . plus work stuff, home stuff, and all the needs of my other two children. I feel the tears coming and try to stop them. I don't want to ruin all the makeup artist's work. I clench my lips tight and widen my eyes. The tears break through anyway. The makeup artist and I make eye contact in the mirror. She puts her hand on my shoulder and gently says, "It's okay. We'll fix it. Don't worry."

The manuscript for my first book is already completed, but I feel a strong need to change the last chapter. I call my literary agent and editor to ask them if it's too late to drop in new material. I'll protect Luka's privacy, but I can't let this book go to print without figuring out a way to somehow address what is happening in my family. I'll prioritize my agreement with my children that I will not publicly say anything about them without their full permission, but I'll find a way to articulate the powerlessness and chaos I'm experiencing so that someone else might read it and feel less alone. Families walking through the same hell as we are will be able to read between the lines.

The last chapter, which used to open with a funny story about a video that went viral, now begins, "I broke down in public recently. . . . Because parenting can break us." This chapter becomes what I need to hear right now.

During the time Luka is living at the residential center, I have two weekends of tour dates scheduled. A year prior, when I was offered a national tour, I agreed to do it under the condition that I would be allowed to pick the dates, and I could do as few as I wanted, with long breaks in between if I chose to. Looking back now, I'm so thankful I didn't overcrowd my schedule.

Now, as I travel out of town for the first of the remaining tour dates, I'm nervous. I keep my phone near me at all times. I don't want to miss Luka's call. I'm not allowed to call him; he has to call me, and he can call only once a day. The day of my show I don't hear from him. I finish my first act, trying really hard to focus on the audience and the show, but I can't stop thinking about Luka. Everything inside me wants to cut the show short and scream: *I can't give you hope because I don't even have enough for my own family right now!* But instead I just keep delivering the jokes and my encouraging message. It's good for me. There's comfort in finding a way to put some good into the world even when I'm at my lowest.

I run backstage after that first act and check my phone. No missed calls. Then, right before I'm about to walk back on-stage for the second act, when the lights are already up and the intro music is playing, my phone starts buzzing. The screen reads "Unknown Caller," which means it is the residential treatment center. I grab it, show it to my tour manager, and say, "Sorry, I'm taking this!" I step into the green room to speak with my son. This call ends up being one of the best talks we have while he is at the center. I'm not sure what the audience thinks about us leaving them sitting in the auditorium for an extra ten minutes, watching an empty lit stage with the same intro song on repeat, but I'm choosing to believe they would do the same if they were in my shoes.

It's impossible to balance all of life's demands. Whenever I try to equally manage every aspect of my life, I end up feeling like I'm trying to balance too many porcelain plates on a serving tray. No matter how carefully I walk, inevitably one or another will fall and smash to pieces. I've learned that balance isn't about doing everything all at once and perfectly. Balance is about choosing each plate in turn—choosing which one needs to move and which one I can put down for a moment. And even though family will always come before work, following through on my commitments and contracts and bills to pay means that sometimes I will have to pick up a plate that I don't want to and, for a bit, put down the one that means more to me. I used to feel guilty about those trade-offs, but I don't anymore.

My children learn how to live by watching me live. My children learn how to treat themselves by watching the way I treat myself. My children learn self-care by watching me taking care of myself. My children learn to prioritize their sanity by watching me prioritize mine.

A few years later I will get to ask Luka what he thinks about the fact that I went through with my birthday party three days after he was hospitalized. "You deserved it, Mom," he'll reply.

And he's right.

The Squeaky Wheel Needs the Most Grease

---⊙---

When Matea was little, she was so brave when it came to jumping into the pool and swimming like a pro, but she wasn't brave about speaking up when she needed to share something personal with me or stand up for herself when she was being treated unfairly by others. So when she was around six years old, I told her, "You know how when you're standing on the diving board, I count one, two, three and then you jump in the pool and you swim and feel so light and free? Well, how about this? When you're struggling to share something important with me, I'll say, 'One, two three, jump!' and then you let your words just jump out of your mouth, knowing that you'll feel so much lighter and more free."

We tried it. She did it. She was able to express herself, and it gave us a chance to talk through all of her big feelings.

The evening when my mother-in-law rushes over to get Matea and Ari after I've called the cops on Luka, the timing could not be worse. Just as they start to pull out of the driveway, a police officer walks out of the house with Luka, who is in handcuffs, and puts him in the back of the police vehicle. Ari, age four, watches through the car window. "Grammy, the policeman is taking Luka away! They're taking Luka away!" Matea, who was fourteen at the time, steps into the role of protective big sister—a role she's sadly taken on too many times over the past few years—and comforts Ari. "It's going to be okay. Don't worry, Ari. Everything will be okay."

She doesn't believe the words coming out of her mouth. She's scared.

I am fully aware that this, along with all the other chaos my younger children have witnessed, will leave a mark on them.

I meet with Luka's therapist, Brian, to ask him for advice regarding my children. Brian tells me to pay attention to any significant changes. Are they sleeping okay? Are their eating habits the same? Are they still enjoying the activities they normally enjoy? Are they still wanting to be around their friends? He advises me to keep communication open but not to focus on Luka's situation unless the kids are bringing it up themselves, and to do all I can to avoid creating any additional stress. Philip and I don't see any changes in their mood or behavior.

The day after Ari witnessed Luka being taken away in a police vehicle, we tried to find an explanation that would be age appropriate for him. We tell him that Luka hasn't been feeling well for a while. He needed to go to the hospital, but instead of the ambulance taking him there, the police officers offered to take him. This is the best I can come up with. And it reinforces my feeling that there needs to be a separate three-digit number people can call when they're having an emergency with a loved one who is struggling with mental health. The police shouldn't have to (and often aren't trained to) deal with these situations. We reassure Ari over and over that Luka isn't in trouble and he's not going to jail. He will be home as soon as the doctors can help him get a little better. Once Luka is transferred from the hospital to the residential treatment center, we tell Ari that he is at a special camp where he is getting even more help to feel better. Ari seems satisfied with our explanations. Occasionally we see him go into Luka's room, hoping he'll find his big brother there. Whenever Luka is mentioned in a conversation, we ask Ari if he has any questions, and the only thing he ever asks is, "When will Luka come home?"

One day, as I'm headed out to visit Luka at the residential center, Ari begs me to bring him along. Luka has been away from home for over a month.

"No, you can't come, buddy, I'm sorry. But I will give him a big hug from you, okay?"

Ari asks if he can make a little video for Luka. I'm not sure the residential center will allow me to show Luka a video on my phone, but I record it anyway. Ari looks straight into the phone camera and in his cute little four-year-old voice says, "Luka, you're the greatest man ever. I love you so much. I wish you'd come back home."

My eyes fill up with tears. "He will come back home. He'll come home as soon as he feels better."

Then Ari runs off to finish building his fort. I can tell he's thinking about his brother a lot.

After more than seven weeks apart, Luka and Ari reunite at the airport, just before our flight to Croatia to visit family.

The instant Ari sees Luka, he runs into his arms. Luka picks him up, Ari wrapping his legs and arms around his big brother as tightly as he can.

Ari's eyes get red and he puts his face in Luka's neck and says, "I missed you so much."

"I missed you too, Ari," Luka says, still holding his little brother in his arms. "I heard you turned five years old two weeks ago! That's so cool!"

My heart is melting watching this exchange between my boys, and I am hoping and praying that this scene right here becomes the more vivid memory in Ari's mind, and that the scene he witnessed of Luka in handcuffs begins to fade as time goes on.

Months later, Philip is trying to get Ari to help clean up his toys, and Ari is refusing to listen. Finally, Philip starts to get frustrated and says, "If I have to ask you again and you don't start cleaning up, you're going to be in trouble." Ari pauses, and looks up at Philip with his big brown eyes. "Daddy, is that when you call the police and they take me away for a very, very, very long time?"

Our sweet little boy was holding that thought, that fear, that stress in his tiny body for weeks, and none of us could see it.

We were checking in. We were paying attention. We were going over the checklist of warning signs to look for. No boxes were checked and none of our care yielded any information. And yet we still missed so much.

When Philip was young, his oldest brother grappled with mental health challenges. For years, Philip witnessed many tense and scary moments that made him concerned for his brother. At ten years old, he watched his brother being taken away in an ambulance following a severe panic attack. The family worried they'd lose him. The sight terrified and over-whelmed Philip. He was unequipped to fully process what he was seeing, but he chose not to bring up any of his concerns. His parents did their best to reassure him that everything was going to be okay and that his brother would be fine. Philip listened and nodded, confirming that he understood. He didn't ask questions. He didn't say a word. That afternoon, Philip had football practice, and because he was aware of the strain his parents were under and didn't want to add more work or stress by asking for a ride, he offered to go alone. Philip grabbed his helmet and hopped on his bike. As soon as he got far enough away from the house so no one could see him, all the emotions he had held in for hours came pouring out. The tears continued until he got close to his destination. Then he quickly wiped his face and composed himself so that no one would know he was upset.

He didn't tell his parents about the tears. He didn't share his worries. He didn't want to burden them. They had enough to deal with so, in his mind, the least he could do was keep his pain and fear to himself. He was determined not to add anything to what they were already going through. It took Philip until he was forty-five years old to finally share with his parents the stress he carried alone as a child. His mom, feeling awful for Philip's silent suffering, asked what she could have done differently so that he would have opened up. Philip reassured her she had done nothing wrong. He always knew his emotions mattered to his parents. It's just that everyone saw Philip as the "good" kid so he convinced himself that he had to play that role, especially during challenging times in the family.

Come to find out, Matea also played that role for a while during the turbulent years with Luka, trying to shield me from any additional stress. There is a unique type of indescribable ache and guilt that floods a parent's soul when we realize that our child is willing to silently carry a heavy burden just to lighten ours.

Not everyone's struggles show themselves in the same ways. Some kids don't have angry outbursts. They aren't disrespectful. They don't lie or steal. They get out of bed. They excel at school. They don't self-medicate. These types of kids are often labeled as the "easy" kid, the "good" kid. The good kid's actions don't require immediate attention. The good kid's demeanor doesn't call for concern. The good kid doesn't elicit worry or fear. And when we as parents already have a child whose behavior is screaming for constant, urgent attention, and we feel like we're at our breaking point, it's comforting to convince ourselves that the other children, the "good" ones, are doing just fine.

But "good" kids struggle too. Sometimes they struggle the most. It's just that they're so used to being praised for being good that they will go out of their way to make sure they're not the ones causing any stress or panic. Often the compliant child takes one for the team. They stuff their pain while their struggles swell and intensify. Kids in our society are applauded for keeping the peace. Very rarely does anyone wonder what maintaining that peace is costing them.

I knew the story about Philip and his brother, and yet I still end up oblivious to so much of what my children are going through beneath their smiles and typical behaviors. It feels like my whole world is crashing. All of my children are struggling in their own way. My marriage is way past struggling and pretty much nonexistent at this point. I feel like I've lost control over every human and every relationship and every bit of peace and sanity in my home. And I wish we could just press pause, then rewind, and start from scratch. Or fast-forward to when everyone and everything are better. I need something, anything, other than the present. The whole goal of trying to live in the moment feels like a bunch of fluffy, useless nonsense right now. I thought I was doing okay navigating everyone's needs. I understand intellectually that each of us has our own unique way of processing fear and stress. I have always tried my best to parent each child with a personalized approach, and yet so much goes undetected. Everything with Luka was so big and loud that I allowed that urgency to drown out everyone else's needs. Luka's words and actions have been screaming for support. Everyone else's words and actions whisper for support.

Instead of just accepting with relief that simple phrase my kids feed me—"I'm okay"—I should have brought up the diving board. I should have counted to three as many times as they needed me to until they were ready for their words to jump out. And then I should have intently listened, not for one second assuming I knew the why or the how. Each of my children deserves my full attention regardless if one is suffering more vividly than the others. Each of my children deserves for me to stand in awe of their story. And yet so often, during this time, I was unintentionally casting Luka as the main character in their individual stories.

I used to think that being a good parent meant I had to be a leader and my kids would follow. I needed to hold their hand and pull in the direction I wanted them to go. I know now that the healthiest way for me to parent is to walk alongside them, paying attention to ways I can best support them on the path they are choosing to travel. And when I screw up, I choose to own my mistake. Not beat myself up, but own it. I need to acknowledge their experience and really hear their point of view. Past or present, I want to mend any wrongdoing. There is no expiration date on my desire to take responsibility and offer an apology when my kids need it. I can't be helpful if I think I know it all. I can be helpful only if I'm continuing to learn.

When one of my kids opens up, I can't try to pull in any specific direction. Instead I must sit as a student listening to an expert. My child is the only expert at being themselves. I am here simply to listen, ask questions, listen more, and then ask, "What is the best thing I can do to help you today?"

We make it a point to ask Ari more questions on a daily basis, trying new ways to get him to open up and talk through his big feelings. But sometimes I'm questioning the questions. I'm worried that all this searching and supervision might actually be creating the anxiety we are trying to detect.

One day, I tell Matea that Philip and I would like to do something with her each week. No one else is invited. Just the three of us hanging out, every single week. I'm not sure how she'll react because she's at an age when spending time with friends is much more exciting than hanging out with your parents. But the instant I suggest the weekly hangouts, Matea's face melts and she tells us she'd really like that.

My first thought is: Why didn't I start this years ago, when so much attention started going to Luka?

My second thought is: More credit than criticism, more grace than judgment. Now is better than never. I am committed to doing better. This applies to my relationship with my children. But it is also true for my marriage.

In an ideal world, going through heartbreak and chaos would bring two people even closer together and connect them on a deeper level, because they are the only ones who can completely understand what the other is going through. But in reality, when a family experiences the turmoil we're stumbling through, the casualty often ends up being the marriage.

Philip and I have a really beautiful love story. I met him as a divorced single mom of two little kids, full of cynicism when it came to love and marriage. Years ago I publicly shared the story of when Philip and I were dating and I called him in the middle of the night because Matea woke up vomiting. The kids were both screaming, everyone was a mess, and I kept thinking, "Why would any man sign up for this?"

So I called Philip, woke him up, and told him that if he thought he wanted me and all my life entailed, he should come over immediately. I wanted to show him what a disaster marrying a single mom would be. I was so nervous about giving marriage another try that maybe I was even subconsciously trying to scare him off. Philip showed up, grabbed the already disgusting rag out of my hand, sent me to bed, and finished cleaning up my daughter's vomit. He tucked Luka and Matea back into bed, then tucked me in, kissed me on the forehead, and said, "Yes, I want this. I want every part of it. All three of you."

When I shared this story in a video and later in my first book, I received endless messages and emails from people who were inspired to not settle for anything less than what they or their children deserve.

Our love story was an inspiration to many. But when life got really hard, we forgot that we were playing for the same team. Our marriage became like that toy a kid begs for and is so excited to receive, but then soon after, the toy ends up shoved in the back of a dresser drawer with no attention paid to it.

During these tough years, Philip and I don't grow apart; we consciously pull apart due to the apathy we feel toward our marriage. Growing distant is a deliberate choice we make. It doesn't happen to us. We are active participants in destroying our close bond. Stress doesn't have the power to ruin a marriage. People have the power to ruin a marriage.

And neither of us has any leftover energy to genuinely

care. Marriage starts to feel like yet another thing on our emotional to-do list, a list that is already suffocating us.

Philip and I are two very different people. In many ways this has benefited our marriage, but dealing with the stress and grief and fear in very different ways can build resentment if there's no open communication. Neither of us does anything terrible, per se, but somewhere along the way, we become roommates, just going through the motions, each processing the fresh new hell we're faced that day on our own. Individually. Always apart. Sometimes we bicker. Often we don't even speak.

We are living in such uncertainty, a new storm raging at every turn. Perhaps staying in our own cocoons feels safer than being vulnerable, even with someone we have been vulnerable with for years.

Throughout this coldness between us, there's an occasional moment that reminds me of the love we once shared. One day after coming back from a meeting, I walk into the bathroom to find Matea lying in a fetal position on the tile floor. She has just thrown up. And who is right next to her, handing her a glass of water and cleaning up her vomit? Philip.

And during moments like those, I think, *I am so fortunate that at this point in my life my burdens are shared. Why am I wasting my one precious life not welcoming that?*

The tension between Philip and me breaks with one simple

conversation months later. We are in our bathroom, completely ignoring each other as we have gotten used to doing. Even small talk is gone at this point. I put my toothbrush down and say, "I feel like you're done. Are you done with this marriage?"

He looks back at me and says, "I don't want to be done. Are you done?"

I know that I don't want to live in a loveless marriage. I know that I don't want to settle. I didn't even plan on getting married ever again after my first marriage ended because I never wanted to be in a bad or even mediocre marriage. But I also wasn't ready to completely give up on Philip and me.

"I'm not done yet," I reply. "I have a suggestion. This might sound weird, but I think we should email each other every day."

There were times when Luka was struggling and I didn't feel like he could hear my words or he flat-out refused to. I would type him a letter, print it out, and give it to him. Reading my words instead of listening to them seemed to help. It gave him the time he needed to absorb what I was trying to tell him, before responding. I decided the same might help my marriage.

For months, Philip and I email each other every single day. It gives us a chance to express all our thoughts, feelings, frustrations, and needs without doing so in the heat of an intense moment. It gives us the time and space to read each other's words over and over again, and really hear what the other person is communicating without immediately becoming defensive. It gives us a chance to reflect and then respond to each other with a lot of thought. The emails dig deep. We pour our souls out—every hurt, every resentment, every unmet need, every complicated feeling, every regret, every mistake, every bit of shame and guilt and fear. We lay it all out. We are processing not just our issues with each other, but our own baggage, digging into our individual histories, the why and how and what of who we are. The emails also allow us to be more present when we're together, and not get bogged down with hashing stuff out and getting into useless arguments. We make an agreement that if we're in the middle of a conversation that isn't productive for one reason or another and one of us says, "Let's email about this," we have to end that conversation immediately and then commit to emailing about the topic at hand within the following twenty-four hours.

The idea to email each other daily is simple. The result has been powerful. Those emails soften and open our hearts. They teach us things about each other we never knew. They bring clarity and empathy. I no longer believe in falling in love. Falling doesn't require much effort and maybe that's the appeal. I believe in building love. These emails help us rebuild our love. They help heal our marriage.

And then Philip and I start dating each other again, finding time to really connect—genuine connection, something I need more of with every member of my family, especially during this time. I need to keep reminding myself that every moment, every interaction with my child or my spouse is an opportunity for connection.

Each of us is hurting. Our relationships with one another are hurting. And though the turmoil surrounding Luka's mental health may have been a catalyst for the manifestation of our personal struggles, it brought to the surface things that might otherwise have stayed buried, repressed, and unspoken, if things had not gotten so out of control. A strong family isn't defined by everything being wonderful and successful. What makes us strong is the messy parts, and the willingness to be honest about our struggles and flaws. Our strength lies in leaning into the disheveled, uncomfortable, complicated stuff and refusing to pretend that things are okay if they're not okay.

It's late afternoon. Luka still hasn't gotten out of bed. I see Matea slip a piece of paper under his bedroom door. It's a note from her that reads: *Don't let the tough days get the best of you. That's what you always say to me. Love, Matea.*

It's evening. Ari has fallen asleep on the couch. Luka picks him up and carries him up the stairs, sweetly whispering, "I got you, buddy." Then he tucks him in.

It's the middle of the night. I'm lying in bed wide awake. Philip can tell my mind is full of worries again. He puts his arm out to pull me closer to him and says, "Wherever you are, don't be there. Come back here. Be with me in the now." I lay my head on his chest and exhale.

We need each other. We fail each other. We rally around each other. We disappoint each other. We love each other.

Lie #7

Information
Leads to Clarity

————⊙————

When we were little, the first time we made our bed all by ourselves, the grown-ups in our life said something like, "Wow! You didn't even ask for help. You did that all by yourself! We're so proud of you."

The first time we tied our shoes, the adults seemed so impressed. "You did that with no help at all! No help! You are so smart and capable."

And as we grew and grew, and accomplished bigger and more difficult tasks, we kept getting praised for doing things all by ourselves, without any help.

And then we got older. And life got complicated. Stressful. Painful. We tried really hard to do it all by ourselves. And it didn't leave us feeling proud. It left us feeling exhausted. And alone.

————⊙————

I'm desperate for clarity. If I can gain more knowledge and gather more information, I'm sure I will be able to figure out how to help Luka get healthier.

And I'm also desperate to stop feeling desperate, to find a quiet place in my mind. To try to wear my brain and my body out a little, I've been working out with my friend Ashley, who is a Pilates instructor. At first all I can handle is the occasional one-on-one session in her garage. I'm awkward. My body is out of shape and I have no clue what I'm doing. Ashley is patient with me and encouraging, and won't let me go home until I've challenged myself.

I never feel like going. I'm always glad I did.

Eventually, I attend group classes at Ashley's Pilates studio, aptly named Grit and Gratitude. Those fifty-minute classes are my escape.

As she's coaching us, trying to motivate us, Ashley will occasionally say something to the class that strikes me. They're just little declarations meant to push us through a challenging move, but they give me a new way to think about my challenges at home. I silently repeat her wisdom over and over in my head during our workouts, and then call on those Ashley-isms in dark moments.

"Keep going. Talk yourself into it."

"Don't focus on the outcome. Focus on what this moment can give you."

"Anything in your mind that's not serving you, let go of."

When we return from our trip to Croatia, I start working on finding Luka a new psychiatrist. While at the hospital and residential treatment center, he was under the care of their doctors. Going back to the doctor he saw before being hospitalized isn't a good option. He still feels betrayed that she shared their private conversation with me, the one where he told her he wasn't willing to give up drugs in order for her to adjust his medication.

Through more phone calls, emails, and research, I track down a seemingly good match. These phone calls, emails, and research have almost become a reflex for me at this point—and a full-time job. And I hate the hustle of it all. When a human is thoroughly stressed out, the last thing they need is a list of stressful assignments with looming deadlines to meet. I wish I had a mental health secretary who could gather all the information regarding Luka's health and place it in one simple file that I could text to a special hotline, which would in turn recommend the perfect doctor and map out the next steps for my son's treatment.

The new psychiatrist is forty-five miles from our home, which in Los Angeles traffic can take anywhere from one to two and a half hours each way. The exasperated part of me just doesn't have patience for the unpredictability of city traffic, and can only see more time away from my other kids as an epic waste. The put-it-in-perspective me looks forward to the one-on-one time I'll get with Luka during the long drives. Some of my favorite conversations with my kids have taken place in the car. Other parents I know feel this way too. There's something about being in a car that makes kids chatty. Maybe it's the fact that they don't have to look a parent straight in the eye, or maybe they're just bored and have nothing better to do in the car, so they talk more than usual.

On our first ride to see the new psychiatrist, I try to get Luka to open up. He's weathered a lot of changes in the past few months. He was hospitalized, moved to a residential center, joined our family trip to Croatia, and then came back to the house with so many complicated memories. He changed schools, plus he's behind because he never completed his sophomore year. I'm worried. I crave some insight into how he's dealing with everything.

I start, a few minutes into our drive, by simply asking how he's feeling. Luka shoots me a dismissive "I don't know." I take a deep breath, let a little time pass, and try again with a more specific question.

"Is there anything you're worried or stressed out about today?"

He doesn't even bother to answer, and I can tell by the way he's holding his body in the seat that he's irritated with me. According to my GPS, we still have an hour and twenty minutes until we reach our destination. It seems like I have plenty of time to get something out of Luka before we arrive at his appointment. But all I get is a son who is really annoyed with me for asking questions instead of just leaving him alone.

The first appointment with the new doctor goes well. He takes a lot of time with Luka and seems very thorough, which is the minimum I expect from someone who will be prescribing my child psychotropic medications. After speaking with both of us and reading through Luka's history, the doctor suggests that Luka complete an evaluation with UCLA's Max Gray Child and Adolescent Mood Disorders Program (CHAMP), a clinical and research service that provides diagnostic evaluations for young people who have symptoms of significant and impairing mood disorders.

I'm excited. This is exactly what we need—more answers.

Through the doctor's recommendation, we are able to get on the waiting list for the program. It takes a few weeks, and then one day I get an email saying a spot suddenly opened up and asking if we can make it the following morning. I cancel everything and take Luka out of school, and we head out on another long drive through Los Angeles traffic, me trying to get Luka to open up, Luka trying to get me to shut up.

We meet Dr. H., a child psychiatrist who will spend a few hours during each step of the evaluation talking to Luka and taking detailed notes, and then present her findings to the team monitoring Luka's case.

At the beginning and end of each long session with Luka, Dr. H. calls me in, either to ask me some questions or to give me an update. During one of those sessions, she lets us know that Luka's diagnosis needs to be updated. In addition to clinical depression, he has generalized anxiety disorder and attention-deficit/hyperactivity disorder (ADHD). She also lets us know that the team at CHAMP has eliminated bipolar disorder, dissociate identity disorder, and a few other diagnoses that had been on their radar for Luka.

Luka's new diagnoses don't surprise me, but I'm annoyed

that he wasn't diagnosed previously so that we could have gotten him help sooner. I'd had a feeling he had ADHD from a young age. I brought it up to his kindergarten teacher, but she didn't seem concerned. She thought of him as just a rowdy kid who needed to learn to sit still. I talked to his pediatrician about it, but she dismissed my concerns, saying, "If he can focus when he wants to, he doesn't have ADHD. Kids who have ADHD can't focus even when they try to." At the time, I was on Medi-Cal, a program in California that offers free or low-cost health coverage to children and adults with limited income and resources. I was a young, insecure mom and instead of trusting my gut, I trusted his teacher and the only doctor I had real access to.

The anxiety diagnosis doesn't shock me either. I could tell Luka seemed stressed out and worried a lot the past few years, but I thought his anxiety was related to his grades sliding, or all the secrets he had been keeping from us with the drug use and stealing.

I am learning through Dr. H. that his severe anxiety might be contributing to the depression and making it worse. Are we finally getting clarity? Are we reaching the top of the mountain? This feels like a huge step in the right direction and I'm hopeful.

During one of Luka's sessions with Dr. H., as I'm sitting in the waiting room, she calls me into the assessment room sooner than I'm expecting and asks Luka to give us some privacy. I sit down in the small room, with Dr. H. sitting across from me. She is kind and wise, and I've grown to trust her.

Dr. H. leans in toward me, the way a friend might who genuinely cares about you.

"Ms. Kuzmič, I have to ask you something. Luka already answered this, but I just have to confirm. . . . Do you have a gun in your home?"

"A gun? No, we don't own a gun."

I don't even have time to process her question before she asks the next one.

"Does Luka go to anybody's house who might have a gun? Do any of your friends' homes have guns?"

"I . . . I don't think so, no. I'm not a hundred percent sure if any of them own guns. I don't know."

She continues, "I need you to think hard if there's any chance he could have access to a gun."

My mind is racing, trying to think of every person Luka is around, every home he might spend time in.

Dr. H. closes her folder of notes, puts it down on the table next to her, looks me in the eye, and says, "If Luka has access to a gun, he will kill himself. He has thought it through. After speaking with him, I am pretty convinced he would have already done so if he had a chance."

Everything suddenly feels blurry. I cannot form a sentence or even a simple thought. Dr. H. is handing me some clarity here, but not the type I'm chasing. This clarity doesn't feel like a path toward healing. She keeps talking, but I can't hear her anymore. I am breathing in not oxygen but pure panic and exhaling any bit of normalcy I still held on to.

I knew that Luka was suicidal, but hearing a doctor—who at this point has gotten to know my son really well—tell me directly that my child would already be dead if he had access to a gun makes our situation feel much more real and grim.

Dr. H. instructs me to put away all the knives in the house. We shouldn't take any risks.

My brain completely shuts off at this point. What is this life we are living? How am I supposed to function with this much fear?

I thought getting the new diagnoses, adjusting the treatment, having new answers would lead to progress. But here I am now taking every knife from my kitchen and hiding it from my child.

Yes, on paper, I have more clarity. But my everyday experience now feels infinitely more chaotic.

At the next Pilates session, during a particularly challenging move I haven't done before, Ashley says, "Meet the moment with ease and truth." As I'm sweating and trying to balance, tears start streaming down my face. It's as if my body is trying to physically release the stress and fear I'm carrying. But I don't know how to do that, how to meet the terrifying moments of my life with ease and truth. Is that even possible?

At the residential treatment center, the staff recommended that Luka continue working in support groups as part of his therapy. They gave us suggestions and I chose the one closest to us. The meetings at this program are three-hour sessions on Monday and Wednesday evenings. Every Saturday morning we attend a three-hour family session together.

The woman leading all the meetings is Jacy. She is in her midthirties and has a captivating presence. One side of her head is shaved, unveiling just one of the many tattoos adorning her body. Strands of vibrant blue highlights run through her hair. Her demeanor is unapologetically bold and blunt, as if she's weathered countless experiences and is now immune to shock.

I observe some parents' apprehension about Jacy. A few don't like the tattoos. Some complain about her language. They question her credentials. Jacy failed sixth, seventh, and eighth grade, and had to attend summer school every year. The first quarter of ninth grade, she dropped out of school entirely. At twenty-eight, she got her GED. In order to lead these support groups, she went through an eight-month training.

But most parents at these meetings, including me, can tell she is exactly who our children need in their life right now. She is a wealth of knowledge—real-life knowledge, the stuff you can't learn from a book but only through surviving personal hell.

Jacy suffered from depression from as early as she can remember. She grew up with a physically and emotionally abusive, alcoholic father. She was in elementary school the first time she attempted suicide. Then, at nine years old, she had to figure out how to process her grandmother's suicide. Her grandmother hanged herself on Jacy's swing set. Jacy was only eleven years old the first time her aunt gave her heroin. She was fifteen years old when she was repeatedly raped and sodomized by her father's crystal meth dealer. After a series of arrests and living in various crack houses, followed by attending numerous support groups, at nineteen, she decided to get sober and has maintained her sobriety. Eventually she started working with teens who are struggling. For the first time in her life she felt useful, like she was good at something, like she had a purpose. Jacy has attended more funerals of teens than she can count (in one year alone, she attended twelve), and yet with each new kid she meets, she sees hope.

From the very first conversation I have with Jacy, I immediately like her. There's an undeniable authenticity that draws me in. When she talks, she is unfiltered and passionate, raw and open about her own struggles, and candid with the kids in a way that meets them where they are. The most obvious thing about Jacy is her heart. She genuinely cares. She wants to help these kids, but she's also fully aware that she has no power to fix anyone or get anyone to follow her lead. They have to want it for themselves.

Our group is made up of kids who range from ages thirteen to seventeen. Some struggle with their mental health and have never self-medicated, but most of them have used drugs or alcohol as a coping mechanism. Some are numbing or escaping by cutting, or with eating disorders. Some of these kids have been sober for a day, some for over a year, and others are still using. Luka is still using. The kids are drug-tested twice a week, and unfortunately, I am never surprised by Luka's test results. He is no longer lying to us about his drug use. And there's nothing I can do to stop him. I do everything in my power to make it harder for him to use, but I can't stop him.

For months, my Saturday mornings are spent in a room of an old building, with fifteen to twenty other families and our fearless leader, Jacy. Sitting in a big circle with Luka on one side of me and my husband or ex-husband or both on the other, for three hours we allow ourselves the freedom to embrace all the emotions we've been trying to hold back, and voice thoughts we never thought we'd have the courage to confess. These sessions are humbling. They're harsh at times. But mostly, they're therapeutic. To hear someone describe the exact scary scenarios we lived through, to hear both the child's and the parent's perspective, is incredibly enlightening and validating.

Jacy is blunt not only with the kids, but with parents too. She doesn't shy away from calling us on our egos, our mistakes, or our stubbornness. She's quick to point out when one of us is enabling our child or, on the other hand, being unfair and much too hard on them.

It's in these sessions that I become fully aware of how little control I actually have. This realization is terrifying. I've done a lot of work on my control issues over the years. I wrote a whole chapter about it in my first book. I could probably give a great presentation on the topic that would leave people inspired to work on shedding their own unhealthy tendencies toward control. And yet it's becoming crystal clear that I do not have this as mastered as I thought. Or maybe I'm able to pull off the skill only when I'm not mid-crisis. Or maybe I'm unwilling to accept that my power is limited. Especially now. Especially when my child is hurting and making dangerous choices.

I have to keep reminding myself to redirect my focus to the things I actually do have control over. Choosing to listen. Choosing to take in every lesson these group sessions offer me. Choosing to meet each moment with ease and truth.

I learn that my trying to get Luka to open up to me during those long drives to his doctor's appointments was torture for him. Sure, the car ride chats might work for some kids, but for kids who struggle the way Luka does, the prompts made him feel trapped. His anxiety suffocates him, and now on top of that he has a mom who keeps trying to get him to open up while he has no freedom to just get up and walk away. Feeling trapped caused him to shut down and withdraw. I had no idea. And as much as it sucks to hear that I've inadvertently alienated him by not considering how he might feel in those moments, I'm so grateful every time Jacy calls me out on things that I need to learn.

Her suggestion to the teens who struggle with anxiety is to come up with three simple things they're willing to talk about in the car, and then be the ones to lead the conversation so they feel like they have some control. Every car ride I find myself hoping Luka will bring up something that will put my mind at ease. Turns out, it's not the actual content of our conversations that calms my worries. It's realizing how lovely it is to talk to him about little things, about other stuff that's on his mind, the stuff that got buried underneath all the heavy stuff.

I also learn from Jacy that while there should be appropriate consequences for certain actions, some of the consequences I had been dishing out were potentially dangerous. In one of the sessions, after the parents of one of the kids openly share that their child repeatedly broke a house rule, so as a result, they took away the child's phone, I am assuming Jacy will praise the parents for following through. Instead, she looks at them and says, "Do you know how many calls I've received in the middle of the night from a kid who is suicidal or about to self-harm or relapse? I once got a call from a kid who had a noose around his neck. Another kid had already taken a bottle of pills, called me, and said, 'Thank you for everything. Good-bye.' I stayed on the phone with him until the ambulance came to take him to the hospital. He's still alive because he made that call. What if those kids didn't have a phone? You think they would have woken up Mommy or Daddy when they're already mad at their parents for who knows what? No. Your kids call me. Or they call a friend. Do not take away their lifeline!"

All I can think about is how many times I took Luka's phone from him as a consequence for something. He could have easily been one of those kids, needing to reach out to someone in a desperate moment. I never take Luka's phone away again. Yet the phone remains a source of conflict and worry. Eventually, we find a compromise that works. We replace Luka's smartphone with a flip phone. The constant allure of the internet is tough even for adults to manage, but it's especially rough for a child and especially a child struggling with mental health and substance abuse.

Every session with Jacy and these families offers me a gift. Sometimes it's the gift of validation. Sometimes it's a new perspective. Often it's healing. Not just individually for Luka and me, but healing of our relationship. When I try to distill the new operating instructions these sessions have given me, it's hard to ignore the fact that the wisdom that has helped me the most also upends a lot of the conventional advice I spent years metabolizing as the only ways to treat illness, or to heal.

Being around people with similar struggles to his, Luka no longer sees himself as different. He is validated. There is a constant reassurance that says, "Oh, you feel that? Yeah, me too."

Healing doesn't happen in isolation.

When someone in the group breaks down in tears, the response is not, "Don't cry." No one is trying to suppress anything or anyone. Luka starts sharing the deepest, messiest parts of himself, ones he never thought he'd voice out loud.

Healing requires vulnerability.

When the group senses that someone is being dishonest or fake, the response is not to let it slide, because the unspoken agreement is: we bring our whole selves here without pretending.

Healing requires authenticity.

Within the confines of that meeting room, there is a palpable aura of unfiltered truth that boldly ventures into deeply uncomfortable territory.

Healing requires discomfort.

When someone in the group says, "I want to kill myself," the response isn't, "No, don't say that!" The response is:

I get it!

I can relate.

I've been there too.

I understand.

I hear you.

I'm glad I'm still here, though. And I'm glad you are.

Healing requires community.

One evening when I arrive home after one of our long drives, Ari is already in bed, but not yet asleep. I walk into his room and snuggle up next to him. He lets out a big yawn, then asks, "Mommy, if you could have any superpower in the whole wide world, what would it be?"

I think for a minute, then reply, "To heal."

Occasionally, on the way home from one of his support groups, Luka mentions to me people from the group who are sober. He talks about them in a positive way, as if he admires them. After a few more weeks, he starts making comments, in passing, about maybe eventually wanting to stop self-medicating. The "maybe eventually" slowly turns into "definitely some-day." It's as if he doesn't trust himself enough yet to give up the thing he believes is keeping him alive, but spending time with these other kids, multiple times each week, is gradually bolstering his confidence.

I start seeing small changes in Luka. If there's an extra support group during the week that he hears about, he attends. Eventually, he's attending support groups or group-related events six to seven evenings a week. And he's excited about them. I know that he still struggles to get out of bed, and on many days, the last thing someone who is severely depressed wants to do is leave the house and show up to a support group. But just forcing himself to make that first step eventually makes him crave more community. It seems to be a new kind of high he's experiencing, the healthy kind one gets from feeling like they've found the people who not only understand them, but want the best for them. The high of finally belonging to something good.

Still, Luka continues to numb with opioids and alcohol.

With his additional diagnoses, his psychotropic medication gets adjusted.

Still, Luka continues to feel suicidal.

Still, I am chasing answers.

In my search, I stumble across something called a pharmacogenomic test. This simple cheek swab test evaluates an individual's DNA to help determine how their body may metabolize or respond to medication. Because psychotropic medications aren't a one-size-fits-all—and because Luka hasn't seen the changes we hoped medication might give us—could this test be the key to more clarity? Luka's psychiatrist is familiar with the test and affirms that it's often useful, but there is no guarantee it will illuminate the best way forward. Plus, the test is expensive and our insurance won't cover it.

At this point, Philip and I have already seriously discussed the possibility of selling our home. All of Luka's doctor's visits, his therapy sessions, and his hospitalization already cost us much more than we ever expected. The only thing that's stressing me out more than our finances at this point is Luka's health. We decide to proceed with the test.

With each new strategy we invest in, I have to confront the uncomfortable reality that as frustrated as I feel, we have access to a much deeper well of resources than many—certainly more than I had when Luka was little. The mere thought of a family being forced to make dreadful compromises when it comes to their child's well-being fills me with rage. I feel fortunate and I feel guilty.

A few weeks later Luka's psychiatrist emails me the test results.

Attached are the genetic testing results. Luka does not have significant gene-drug interactions that could help guide us.

In other words, the test is a waste of time. There's no additional clarity. Another dead end.

Maybe what makes humans so remarkable is how messy and knotty and mystifying and fuzzy and painful our existence is—even the most educated experts can't fully grasp the complexity that is us. We are a mosaic of biology and circumstance and experience. I know all this, but the mystery of it doesn't seem wonderfully magical to me right now. It seems terrifying.

Four months have passed with Luka attending support groups, and it's Thanksgiving. At his grandparents' home, Luka searches the medicine cabinet and finds a bottle of hydrocodone that his uncle was prescribed after an injury. He steals the bottle. At this point, not much shocks me, but I am freshly alarmed that he is willing to steal from people I know he loves, people who aren't just us. Once again, in what feels like a cruel game of How Many Times Can We Crush a Parent's Hope, I must accept that ultimately I have no control over my son's choices. No one stops doing drugs because their mommy told them to or because she dished out yet another consequence. The decision to get healthy lies solely in Luka's hands. All I can do is wait. Wait proactively.

The week after Thanksgiving, Luka shows up to school, and the guy he gave money to for weed flakes on him. He's frantic and desperate, and the desire to self-medicate blots out every other feeling he has. A few hours later, he is sitting in class and he's struck by the realization that even though he is dead afraid of needles, he would shoot up heroin right now if he could. Suddenly all the stories he's heard in those support groups, all the lessons he's been taking in, all the seeds that have been planted flood his mind. *There's something very wrong. I have a problem. I can continue to pretend I don't, but I'm voluntarily going to support groups almost every day. I'm relating to all those people for a reason. And even when I am high, I'm still really lonely. I'm still miserable. I'm still depressed. Something has to change. I can't do this anymore.*

That evening, Luka attends the Monday night group led by Jacy. Philip heads out to pick him up. They're usually back by nine thirty, but it's eleven and they're still not home. I call Philip, panicked, because by this point, panic has become my standard reaction. Philip doesn't pick up the phone, but he sends me a text letting me know they've been sitting in the garage this whole time, talking. I decide to go to bed knowing that Luka is in good hands.

Luka has always felt close to Philip. I credit Philip with this. He's consistently treated Luka and Matea with respect and value and unconditional love. I once asked Luka if he thought my divorce from his dad contributed to his depression. He replied, "No, because if you hadn't divorced, I never would have had Philip in my life."

Around midnight, Philip wakes me and asks me to come downstairs.

I'm immediately alert and spring down, only to find Luka waiting for me at the bottom of the staircase. He reaches toward me and dumps pills and drug paraphernalia into my hands. I stand frozen, and he looks me in the eyes. Calmly and clearly, he says, "I'm done."

I have been convinced that more evaluations, more tests, more doctors, more experts would be our one and only path to healing. But healing started showing up in an old building among people as lost and as frightened and as flawed as we are.

Lie #8

Breaking Bad Habits Equals Instant Relief

<hr />

When Luka and Matea were toddlers, their dad and I divorced, and the kids and I moved into a small rental apartment. They slept in bunk beds my friend purchased for them, and I slept on the floor next to their bed. One morning, Luka woke us both up around two o'clock because he'd wet the bed. I was exhausted from not just the second job I'd taken, but also the sheer emotional resilience it took to make it through each day. I was too tired to change his bedding, so instead I cleaned him up, put him in fresh pajamas, and suggested, "How about you sleep with me tonight?" He snuggled up next to me. I grabbed his little hand. "Of all the boys in the whole wide world, how did I get so lucky to be *your* mom? I love you so, so, so, so much—do neba visoko!"

He smiled. "I love you too, Mommy."

*T*he morning after Luka decides to stop numbing with drugs and alcohol, his first thought is, *What. Did. I. Do?* But he convinces himself to just make it through that one day. He can numb again tomorrow. Then tomorrow comes and he decides to give it one more day. He jokes that being a procrastinator is coming in handy.

Luka asks us to please take him out of school and let him do an independent program. He explains that he doesn't want the temptation of being around the same kids he used drugs with. I find a charter school in our area for students who, for one reason or another, need a nontraditional learning environment. They offer a flexible program with online courses and weekly in-person meetings with teachers. In a way, the setup is similar to homeschooling.

The idea of him not going to a traditional school feels messy to me. He hasn't been self-motivated and this program requires that discipline. The hours he used to be at school, he is now spending at home and, selfishly, I need those breaks from Luka. Choosing not to self-medicate means that he's given up a way to numb and escape, so he's taking his pain out on me even more than before. What I learned through support groups with Jacy is that for those people who self-medicate, drugs are not the problem. The problem is how they're feeling inside. Drugs, in their eyes, are the solution to that problem. Luka gave up his solution.

On the outside, I am the epitome of a supportive mom, Luka's greatest cheerleader, who is excited that Luka is giving up his unhealthy coping mechanisms. But on the inside, I feel uneasy, doubting him. On the outside, to anyone who knows that Luka has given up self-medicating, he is the epitome of strength. But on the inside, I know he is feeling unsteady.

I never express my doubts out loud. I feel guilty even having them. But after everything we've been through together, I no longer trust him. It's not that I don't have faith in his ability or that I'm not proud of him. It's that I don't have faith in his awareness of the gravity of this situation. I'm also aware that my doubts protect me. I expect the worst in order to avoid being blindsided by yet another heartbreak.

Luka is still getting drug-tested twice a week at the support groups with Jacy. On Saturday, when parents join the group, she has a parent go into the restroom with their child to make sure the child isn't trying to cheat the urine test.

Luka keeps passing each drug test.

I am exhilarated and relieved, but the next few months turn out to be some of the hardest. He's in a lot of emotional pain. I zigzag between worrying that he will relapse and worrying that staying sober right now is too much for his depression and that I will lose him. I find myself shifting from being so incredibly proud to being so incredibly discouraged. It's a serious case of whiplash.

He slams the door in my face.

But also, he hasn't self-medicated for an entire week.

He is completely ignoring his schoolwork.

But also, he is continuing to attend support groups, sometimes six or seven days a week.

He acts really hateful toward his sister.

But also, he finds a healthy hobby to commit to and starts taking piano lessons.

His knuckles are bloody from punching the shower tiles again.

But also, he reaches one month without using drugs or alcohol.

He gets angry at me, starts pulling his hair and punching himself.

But also, I hear from other families in Jacy's group how empathetic and supportive Luka is with their kids.

He doesn't shower or brush his teeth for days.

But also, he starts working out with a boxing coach in our area and feels really good afterward.

He gets in my face and tells me to fuck off.

But also, he hasn't used drugs or alcohol for three months now.

This period is in some ways almost more confusing than when Luka was self-medicating, because when he was using drugs, failing school, being disrespectful, and not taking care of his responsibilities, I could just put everything concerning Luka in a box labeled "Needs to be solved!" And now there are these two separate boxes: on one hand he is choosing to be healthy and that takes a lot of grit and self-control, and on the other hand he still makes decisions that are incredibly unhealthy and destructive to him and the people around him.

Then COVID hits and everything shuts down.

I have been trying to juggle all of my responsibilities, but now there's the added pressure of trying to manage this new world of Zoom school for my children, helping them navigate their own emotions while isolated from their activities and friends. There were already a lot of variables up in the air for our family, but now those and a bunch of new variables hang in uncertainty, with no definitive resolution in sight. My own mental health takes a hit. Stability seems elusive. We're all in the same boat, so I no longer feel comfortable leaning on friends, and I hate that I don't have any bandwidth to offer anyone either. We find ourselves siloed off from one another, confused, nervous in the face of this new normal that we as parents are all trying to adjust to.

The past few years, supporting Luka while trying to also stay present for all the other people and aspects of my life felt like a game of chess in which I examined each piece meticulously as I contemplated every move. I knew the game was complicated, but I just never imagined someone could pull the entire board out from under the pieces.

Thankfully, one of Luka's groups starts meeting virtually. And Jacy gets creative with outdoor meetings, each family sitting six feet apart from the others. Those relationships he has built through the groups are strong and can weather these changes. The kids text one another to check in, to encourage one another, and to hold one another accountable.

Back on the home front, my daily interactions with Luka start off positively. I am determined not to be reactive.

8 a.m.—I walk into his room and speak to him calmly and kindly. I try to encourage him to get out of bed, to start his day off with something fun and then begin his schoolwork.

9 a.m.—I walk into his room. He is still in bed. My tone has shifted to slightly irritated. I turn on his light and leave his door open, letting him know that he needs to get up and start his day.

10 a.m.—I walk into his room. He is still in bed. I can feel all patience leaving my body. My tone is full of annoyance.

11 a.m.—I walk into his room. He is still in bed. I accuse him of not even trying. He snaps back in a sarcastic tone, "Yeah, thanks. I'm not even trying! I'm never trying. I'm a loser. Thanks, Mom." This leads to an unproductive back-and-forth in which I explain to him that I believe in him but he needs to put in effort, and he yells at me to get out of his room.

12 p.m.—I walk into his room. He is still in bed. I take the covers off him. "You have to get up, Luka!" He

screams at me to give him his blankets back and to just fucking leave him alone.

1 p.m.—I walk into his room. He is still in bed. I threaten him with a consequence, like not being able to spend time with the girl he's been dating unless he gets up within five minutes and starts his schoolwork. He gets out of bed, slams the door on me, and then gets back in bed.

How do I know where the line is between laziness and illness? How do I know which behaviors are variables that deserve my empathy and some leeway and which aspects of our interactions are just antagonistic—the part of him that's trying to get one past me, or is pushing my boundaries to see if he can trust me to be strong and steady? It feels impossible in the heat of these moments to discern the difference between the two, and the uncertainty might just be the most frustrating part of the current process. Underneath my sadness and exasperation, I'm also really angry. At times, I don't even like him. And, wow, is that feeling coated with guilt. *I don't even like my own child.*

One afternoon, after yet another round of this fruitless routine—a routine that I'm worried I'll repeat every day, without any clear sign that my efforts are helping—I shut myself in a bathroom. I close the door, slide down to the floor, and surrender to the weight of my heavy emotions. I push the palms of my hands into my temples and stare into nothing. A single thought blares on repeat in my head: *I don't know how to parent a child with mental illness.* My brain is like a radio now tuned to loud static, and tears flow down my face.

I have been told not to baby him or enable him. We have to have rules and boundaries. He has to have some responsibilities. We need to keep encouraging him to finish high school. Yet every time I try to hold him accountable, he either explodes or shuts down. And then I start questioning whether I'm pushing him too hard—pushing him toward hurting himself. Or does all this pushing give him something firm to lean on?

I have attended support groups. I have listened to advice from doctors and therapists. I have participated in parenting courses. I have clocked more time learning about raising a teen with mental illness than anyone else I personally know. I should be an expert at this by now. Instead, I remain clueless.

I'm continually asking myself: *What am I doing wrong? Why can't I figure out a better solution? Why do solutions that work for other kids and families not work for mine? Why can't I figure out a way to motivate him? Am I communicating clearly enough with him? Is it too late? Am I doing enough? Am I doing too much? Will he ever be okay? Why don't I know how to parent my own child?*

I force myself to take a breath. I try to quiet my thoughts. Then something that Ashley said floats to the surface of my mind: "Your job is to stay intentional and connected to peace and love." I pull myself up off the floor. Even though I don't have any confidence that I know what I'm doing, I force myself to follow her words and get back to it. It's the only advice that makes sense right now.

One day, I notice a note on Luka's desk. It's a list that he's written for himself of all the things he's trying to improve on. Everything I've been saying to him is on that list. *Do my homework every day. Brush my teeth. Get up before 9:30 am.*

My shoulders slump with a hit of sadness. I stare at that list and realize that Luka doesn't need me incessantly drilling his responsibilities into him. He's aware of what he needs to do. My nagging and reminding are not teaching him anything new. Reiterating something he already knows only amplifies his feelings of inadequacy by repeatedly shining a spotlight over and over again on the areas where he's falling short. He might act like he hates me, but all my "helpfulness" is actually making him hate himself more and more.

That simple list starts to shift my perspective. I feel like I've been playing a mystery game and I've finally uncovered an essential clue. All his life, Luka has been silently metabolizing my guidance and advice, and he already knows what he needs to do.

My point of view: He's not getting out of bed, so he's not even trying.

His reality: His depression and anxiety are physically draining. He feels like he has no energy to move.

My point of view: He's being completely irresponsible about schoolwork.

His reality: He's so mentally exhausted that he can't concentrate at all, so even attempting to focus on school assignments makes him feel like a failure.

My point of view: He acts like he doesn't care.

His reality: All his motivation and energy are directed toward just trying to stay alive.

It's like I've been asking someone with a broken leg to run.

A year has now passed since Luka stopped using drugs as a coping mechanism. We all numb from time to time. We all look for the fix that will offer instant relief. Something to help us feel in control, make the tough parts more bearable. Everyone's poison may not be the same, yet we all know what it feels like when we've failed to exercise restraint. Luka has done this work consistently for a whole year. It's important to acknowledge the milestone—especially since this kind of success can often come with negative stigma. So I surprise him with a one-year celebration and make him a cake with the image of Mr. Clean on it. I can tell this gesture means something to him, and I'm glad. He shouldn't feel anything but proud.

What's my poison? I find myself wondering. I decide to follow Luka's lead. If he can evolve, so can I. I start asking myself what I need to give up.

The first one is obvious: matching my angry tone to his. No one forces me to take the bait in my interactions with him. But I repeatedly choose to express my frustration in an unproductive way. I insist on having the last word. I attempt to steady everything that feels unsteady. I make many unhealthy choices.

Instead of trying to control everyone and everything, I want to redirect that effort inward. I want to make better choices.

I'm reminded of something Ashley often says when I'm not challenging myself enough during a workout: "Stop running back to what's familiar."

I start practicing taking a deep breath before speaking. I draw strength from the stillness briefly provided by the inhale and the exhale. Often, old habits suck me in. What's familiar feels more comfortable, even when it's unhealthy. And every single time I fail to respond in a productive way, the outcome is predictable. It's almost comical how tough it is for a college-educated so-called grown-up who has well over forty years of life experience and many, many, many therapy sessions under her belt to simply do what she knows is right. How many times have I said to my kids, "You know better!" And yet I fall into the same old patterns, even though . . . I know better.

One evening as I'm passing Luka in the hall, I sense that something isn't right. I catch a glimpse of his forearm and pause in my tracks. I catch him before he can walk past me, and I gently push up his sleeve. There are bloody marks on his arm. Luka has been cutting. A wave of panic crashes over me.

I've learned enough from Jacy at this point to know that screaming, "What were you thinking? You can't do that!" isn't going to be helpful.

I make the choice to do what feels completely counterintuitive and just stay calm. I take a deep breath. I tell Luka that I'll meet him in his room. He nods. I'm so thankful we're at a place where he isn't pushing back against me at every turn. I grab the first-aid kit and sit down next to him on his bed. As I'm putting Bactine on Luka's cuts I notice how shaky my hands are. His gaze is fixed on the floor, and his face is expressionless. Everything within me wants to strongly express how much he has scared me and how he must never, ever do this again! I remind myself to slow down my breath. With a soft tone, though still completely rattled on the inside, I ask him, "What did it feel like? Did it take away your depression?"

"No, it didn't," he quietly replies.

I take another deep breath. "Okay, so how about we decide not to try that again. It didn't work."

I'm still speaking calmly, but it feels as if I'm right on the edge, about to slip and fall into a familiar pattern and lose control over the pace and volume of my words. My heart is beating so fast it feels like it might crash right through my ribs if I don't express the intensity of my fear.

But I take another deep breath. "How about next time, when you're about to do something to try to feel better, talk to me first. Or if you don't want to talk to me, call your therapist or Jacy or a friend. And then one of us can help you figure out another way to cope."

Luka nods. "Okay." And thankfully, he never tries cutting again.

Later that night, as I'm coming down from the adrenaline rush of caring for his wounds, I reflect on the fact that I was able to make my point successfully just by asking a question. Staying calm and speaking softly felt unnatural in the moment, yet by changing my pace and my tone I was able to express my true feelings without triggering a negative outburst—in either of us. I was learning to coexist with my feelings without allowing them to throw me off balance.

One day, Luka points out to me that I used to be a much more consistent parent when it came to my rules, and that the past few weeks or so my consistency has wavered.

"Isn't that a bad thing as far as parenting goes?" he asks me.

After I get over my gut reaction about my kid judging my parenting, I can see that not only is Luka right, but his observation is proof positive that I've been putting in the work and trying to evolve in my parenting. "That's about me learning to pivot."

I was taught that consistency is crucial no matter what, and that changing course leads to confusion. But always driving forward with conviction isn't powerful. Staying nimble is. While the love, support, and commitment need to stay consistent, the path may require pivoting. Getting this right hinges on the correct blend of stubbornness and flexibility. I have to be stubborn about the overall goal and purpose, but flexible in my approach and process.

If I ask Luka to take care of certain chores before the following day, and then the following day I notice his mental health is at a serious low, it would be cruel of me to insist he still take care of everything on the list. So I do my best to encourage him to get out of bed and at least take care of a few small tasks that will make him feel proud of himself and help him push forward. The big tasks can wait a few days.

I make a conscious effort to set aside my agenda and stay open. He needs me to get off his back, and to stand by his side. When he confides in me about something stressful or sad, I refrain from immediately jumping in to try to "fix" it or comfort him. Instead, I choose (on successful days) to simply ask: "Do you want me to just listen or do you want my advice?" I didn't come up with this tactic. I'm not sure where I first heard it, but it works. Giving him agency helps him feel respected, which also fosters a sense of comfort in continuing to open up to me. Most of the time he tells me he just wants me to listen. I sit quietly, feeling beads of sweat forming as I restrain myself from blurting out advice or instructions. Mothers who succeed at keeping their mouth shut the entire time their teenager is opening up to them deserve the Nobel Peace Prize. Almost every time Luka tells me to just listen, eventually (sometimes within minutes, sometimes hours later) he asks for my input.

I am reminded of a lesson I learned at the beginning of this journey: Choose to come from a place of curiosity. It's about the power of questions. People who feel the urge to control are better at statements, but statements aren't always helpful. I am working on being a better listener.

And then there are days when I abandon all the lessons I've learned and repeat my unhealthy choices. Predictably, my old approach always fails us and neither Luka nor I can actually hear the other. I've gotten better at recognizing avalanches like these and stopping before things escalate by suggesting we take a pause. I type what I'm trying to communicate with him, print it out, and offer it to him. "Whenever you're open to it, please read this." Sometimes he reads my note within minutes, and other times it takes hours, but eventually he finds me and we manage to engage in a productive and calm conversation.

The changes I'm making aren't curing Luka. They're not a solution to his lack of motivation. But they're reducing the tension. They are helping us work together. Our communication is improving. Occasionally after an outburst directed at me in the morning, I receive an email from Luka. The simple note usually says: *I am sorry for being mean and yelling this morning.*

We're both working on breaking old habits.

Ashleyism: "Right when it feels too hard, keep going. Change doesn't happen when you're comfortable."

Later that year at Christmas dinner, everyone is taking a turn saying something they're grateful for. We all give familiar answers, with everyone mentioning the usual things: friends, family, good health . . . Until it's Luka's turn. He looks at me and says, "Second chances. I'm grateful for second chances."

Me too.

Every once in a while there's a day when I sense that he's really motivated to better his mental health. He puts in so much effort to get up, to shower, to complete an assignment, to help around the house. Sometimes the effort makes him feel better. Other times it changes nothing, and on those days he withdraws.

One evening, Luka and I are alone in our kitchen. I can tell that he's retreated to that dark place within his mind where everything seems hopeless. I am asking him how I can support him. He paces anxiously back and forth, distraught, unable to find a sense of peace.

"Mom, I can't do this anymore. I'm trying, but things just don't seem to be getting better."

My heart drops. I've heard these words from him before.

"Luka, you won't always feel like this. It will get better."

"It won't!" he snaps back. "You keep saying that, but it won't."

"Luka, it's not just something I say. I really believe it."

"Mom, I have everything a person should need to be happy and I'm never happy! I have parents who love me, I have friends, I have a girlfriend who is amazing, I have all the things I need. But I can't think of anything in the future that would be worth living for. I can't think of a career, or a type of life, or anything that would help me stop feeling this shitty." As he's speaking, his voice quivers, getting shaky, and tears start to pool in his eyes.

"Luka, we will get you more help."

"What more can anyone do? We've done everything. I'm in therapy, I'm on meds, I've been off drugs for over a year. Nothing is working."

"You have had some really good days and there will be more."

"Yeah, sure, sometimes I feel better for short moments, but most days, most of the time nothing is really working."

I find myself uttering words I've said to him countless times before. I can't seem to find new ones. "Luka, you won't feel this way forever. Please believe me."

Every time he's suicidal, I reassure him that this will pass, but how long can you tell someone something will pass before they stop believing you, before their patience wears thin?

At this point, through all the support groups, I've heard too many stories of kids who stopped believing their dark days would pass, and are now gone.

Luka stops pacing and mumbles something through his tears. "I wish you . . ."

"I didn't understand the last part of your sentence, Luka. You wish what?"

"I wish you . . ." As the words are coming out of his mouth, he breaks into a heart-wrenching sob. "I wish you didn't love me."

I am trying to process his words, but I can't figure out what he's trying to tell me.

"Luka, why would you wish that? I could never stop loving you."

"I wish you didn't . . . because then I could just . . . I could just do it. I could kill myself."

I don't move. I don't speak. I struggle under the weight of his words. A raw and overwhelming pain wraps its vines around me as I watch my boy, sobbing, full of anguish and hopelessness, wanting to die but not wanting his death to hurt anyone.

I walk over to Luka, embrace him, and hold him as long as he lets me. I want to say the right thing, but nothing feels right. I try to steady my racing thoughts and ground myself. I allow words to flow from my mouth, fully aware that each syllable carries a great weight—a fear, a hope. "I'm not giving up on you, Luka, but I need your help. I need you to not give up on yourself either, okay? I don't want you to just live. I want you to *want* to live. I understand that you don't believe you'll ever get to that place, but I do. And I'm asking you to please trust me."

He doesn't respond.

I want some sort of a money-back guarantee, except instead of money, can it be a hope-back guarantee? Can I please have my hope back? Can I go back to the time when I genuinely believed that all this professional help would actually make a lasting difference?

I start pleading with him. "Please, Luka. Please hold on. Let's figure out what else we can do to help you feel better. Please."

I remember begging him to please go to sleep when he was a hyper toddler, or to please eat another bite of green beans at dinner, and now I wish that's all I was begging for instead of begging him to please stick around.

A lullaby won't fix this. Bribing him won't fix this.

I can't fix this.

I don't feel safe leaving him alone in his room for the night. I'm scared to let him out of my sight. "Would you sleep in my bed tonight?" I ask, expecting him to reject my offer. Instead, he nods, tears still streaming down his flushed cheeks.

I need him next to me for his own safety. I need him next

to me for my own peace. Philip gladly takes the couch. He understands the gravity of the situation.

I lie next to my seventeen-year-old son, with him on his back and me on my side facing him.

I can see the tension in his body slowly surrendering to soothing ease, as if the weight of his pain has temporarily been lifted off his shoulders. His eyes get heavy. His breathing slows down.

Never could I have imagined that the precious little boy I gave life to would someday not want it.

My mind is going through all the options, attempting to problem-solve, creating checklists for what needs to happen next. I have less than seven months left before Luka turns eighteen, and then I'll lose a lot of power as far as getting him help. I will no longer be able to enroll him in programs. I will not have access to his psychiatrist or be privy to decisions made about his health. I feel the clock ticking, my mind entangled in a whirlwind of racing thoughts: *I haven't done enough! I feel like I've done everything, yet I haven't done enough.*

I push aside the thoughts of doing and fixing and controlling. Instead, I choose to connect.

As I'm watching Luka fall asleep beside me, I grab his hand and say, "I love you so much. Do neba visoko."

He is half asleep, but he squeezes my hand and replies, "I love you too, Mom. Do neba visoko."

Lie #9

Mother Knows Best

———◇———

In a podcast interview a few years back I was asked to describe parenting in one word. I blurted out, "Chopped!" thinking immediately of the popular Food Network show.

In each episode of *Chopped*, four contestants (sometimes professional chefs, sometimes amateurs) are handed a mystery basket of random ingredients and asked to make a delicious meal incorporating every item in the basket. The ingredients range from exotic vegetables most people have never heard of to gummy bear candies to actual bull testicles. Each episode consists of three rounds, and in each round the contestant with the worst-tasting meal is eliminated by the judges. Every time the baskets are opened, the camera zooms in on the contestants—all look shocked or disappointed or stressed out by the ingredients. Some start sweating, while others can't help but laugh at the absurdity of it all. Then we watch the contestants running around the kitchen trying to pull together a great dish, so frazzled that they occasionally drop things or burn whatever concoction they forgot they left on the stove, constantly questioning the choices they're making, continually feeling a step behind, sneaking a peek at what the other contestants are doing to see if they have a better plan, fearing the imminent judgment they'll face for the decisions they've made—all the while determined to complete the task the best they know how. All the while worried they're failing.

Tell me the difference between this show and parenting. You can't.

I'm feeling desperate again and I need Luka to be safe—even if that means we have to take some extreme measures.

"Luka, Philip, your dad, and I talked and we think it would be good for us to find a residential program for you, a place where you can be immersed in getting better with no distractions. How do you feel about that?"

The last thing I want is for him to be away from me again, but I don't know what else to do.

Luka responds with anger and storms into his bedroom to call Sara, his girlfriend.

Sara and Luka met at a support group and were friends for a while before starting to date.

Someone once asked me if I was worried about him dating a

girl who is also struggling. But I'm happy he's seeing someone who is attending support groups and actually putting in the time and energy to prioritize her health. We all struggle at some point.

When Luka calls Sara to tell her about my suggestion, that he might have to go away for six to seven weeks and they won't be able to talk or text during that time, he's mad and nervous. He's not sure how she'll react. I'm nervous too. When I was sixteen years old, if my boyfriend had told me he'd be going away for a long time and couldn't even talk to me or text me for all those weeks, I probably would have been selfish and whined about it.

Sara hears Luka out, then says, "This will be so good for you! I'm excited for you. If anything it will make everything better not just for you, but for us and our relationship. People used to go to war without being able to call each other and they would just write letters. You're going to a place where you can focus on your health. We'll write letters, and I'll be here for you when you get back. This will be the best thing for you, Luka."

I will forever have a special place in my heart for Sara because of the way she handled that conversation and the weeks that followed. I credit her with Luka's willingness to go. She didn't try to control the situation. She let it be. Luka and Sara wrote letters to each other, and she came over to my house every weekend to hang out with our family because, as she put it, we made her feel closer to him.

This residential treatment center we've found is a seven-hour drive from our house. On the way there, it's just Luka and me in the car, and he's in a surprisingly good mood.

"I'm going to make the best of this, Mom. Since I have to do this again, I might as well get the most I can out of everything they offer at the program."

I am fully aware that being this positive is a challenge for Luka, especially when he's shared that suicidal thoughts are still creeping in regularly. I admire him.

Saying goodbye to him this time is even harder than before. COVID restrictions are in full force now, so I won't be allowed to visit him but at least I will see him once a week over Zoom for the family therapy sessions. I give him a big hug. It feels really good to know that both of us are finally and fully aware that we are playing on the same team.

My eyes well up with tears as I say goodbye to him. "I have watched you work so hard to give up coping with drugs and alcohol. I have watched you drag yourself out of bed, and commit to therapy and support groups. I have watched you be vulnerable and open. I have watched you ditch the shame regarding your mental health struggles. Luka, I have no doubts when it comes to your ability to get whatever you need from these next few weeks."

We hold on to each other for a bit, and then I have to let go. I have to get back in the car and drive home without him, hoping that some of the positivity he's worked so hard to cultivate will rub off on me.

Luka thrives in this residential program. And after seven weeks he comes home. He's not depression-free. He's not anxiety-free. But he is better. We are better. Our relationship is stronger than ever. All the seeds that have been planted over the years are sprouting into a new will for life and a new commitment to health. On bad days, he can rely on healthy coping skills he's learned. Sometimes he applies them. Sometimes he doesn't. The path toward health is intricate, often leading us through uncharted territory. Good mental health isn't a destination we reach, and then we've arrived. It's a tension we negotiate day by day.

Now that he's back home and feeling more stable, Luka continues to work on finishing high school. He gets a job and starts saving money. He is asked to share his story at a few groups, and even though he doesn't love speaking in public, he shares. He turns eighteen. He is finally on medication that seems to be helping. He laughs. It has been years since I heard him genuinely laugh. He gets his driver's license and has socked away enough money for a down payment on a used car. We still fall into old patterns. We apologize. We forgive. He has good days and bad days, but most important, he wants to live.

Occasionally, we go backward. We progress. Then we regress. But no lesson is wasted. Some days kicking ass looks like barely holding on. And that's okay. The more I see the overall arc of his journey bending toward self-discovery, autonomy, and progress, the more aware I am of the steps I need to take to move myself forward too. I wish I had realized from the first day I became a mom that parenting should be time spent learning and growing and evolving along with my kids, with grace and patience and kindness not only toward them, but just as important, toward myself.

Luka decides to start working out again with his old boxing coach. They haven't talked in over a year. After their first training session back, I get a text from the coach: *I'm so happy right now. Not to get too dark, but to be honest, I was afraid I'd never see Luka again.*

Every so often, a fellow parent asks me, "What was the turning point for Luka, and for your relationship?"

I know what these other parents want to hear, and I know the yearning behind the question: They want advice. They want reassurance that Luka is okay, that I'm okay, because they hope that means that their family will be okay too. They want clear road signs and landmarks to look out for—signs that say danger, and signs that tell us we've made it through the danger. The truth is, there wasn't one turning point. There were many.

"But when did you notice things between the two of you starting to get better?" these same parents insist. In response, I'm tempted to list all the things I did to try to help him— because I really did try. I tried so hard. But the answer is both much simpler and much more complicated than a catalog of my efforts. Things really began to improve, little by little, when instead of trying to fix Luka, I worked on myself.

And that's it. That's the big secret, the mysterious key I searched for yet held in my hand the entire time. Yes, all the research, all the professional help we received, the support groups we attended—those resources were extremely beneficial and we were fortunate to have access to them. But all that help didn't turn me into a better support system for Luka. What helped us most was me choosing to shine a light on the unhealed parts of myself that I brought into my parenting.

Since childhood, the world has insisted that the people around me know what is best for me—and I took that insistence to heart. The power structures around me—society, culture, traditions, norms, organized religion—decided on an ideal framework, and I found myself still bound up in this framework thinking things like, *This way is right. This is what success looks like and this is what failure looks like. These are the rules. This is the timeline we follow. This is the way we parent. This is how we handle struggles. This is what we believe in. This is who we are.*

I felt guilty when I shouldn't have. I exhausted myself trying to make sure we ticked every box. I worked so hard trying to mold my family to the framework that I started to believe *we* were the problem.

Each time I've made a choice, in my parenting or otherwise, that deviated from the "ideal," I have felt like a disobedient little child, expecting to be met with criticism. *That's not okay. That's not how we do things. That's not normal in our family/church/society.*

So many of the decisions I made in life were motivated by a need to prove that I'm enough to people who happen to be just as imperfect and lost as I am. It's hard to be a good parent when you're chasing someone else's definition of good.

In one of Ashley's classes, she has us stand on the Pilates reformers in some inhumane position that is really challenging my balance and testing my strength. I'm looking straight ahead, focused. Deep breath in. Deep breath out. As my endurance wanes, my thoughts turn from *I can do this* to *Am I doing it right? Is it this hard for everyone else too? Am I the only one starting to shake?*

In a moment of doubt, I turn my head to assess the people next to me. And the instant I look over, I completely lose my balance and fall off the reformer. I pick myself back up and laugh. It dawns on me that every time I have lost my balance, it has been because I shifted my focus from my own practice to compare myself to someone else. In Pilates. And, it turns out, in every other aspect of my life too.

As I get back on the reformer, Ashley yells over to me, "Trust yourself!"

I leave class thinking about her words. How can I trust myself when I'm not an expert at Pilates? How can I trust myself when this is a completely new move for me? But Ashley isn't telling me to trust that I'll execute the move perfectly, with impeccable form. She is telling me to trust that I know my body, to trust that I know my own ability, to trust that I'm aware of my own strengths and weaknesses, to trust myself without looking for everyone and everything else to tell me who I am or what I should do or what I'm capable of.

Trusting myself means trusting that I'll know when I don't know, that I'll be aware of areas where I need to seek out wisdom, and that I'll choose the right people to help me. She's telling me to trust my own values.

Three years before, early into me finding out Luka was struggling, he had a sporting event at his school. He didn't want to go, but I talked him into it. He was severely depressed that day and I was hoping that getting out of the house, being outside, and doing something active with his peers might help a little. After the game, as I was watching Luka walk across the field toward me, his head down, looking defeated despite the fact that his team had won the game, a woman walked up to me. "Hi! I follow you on social media. Oh my goodness, I just love you! I want to tell you how much your videos have helped me, but first can I have a photo with you?" In the past, I would've said yes to this well-meaning stranger. I have always gladly said yes to these types of requests. But saying yes just didn't feel right in that moment. My son was having a hard day. It felt weird to be posing for a photo in front of him or making him wait while this woman praised my videos. So I took a deep breath and did something I've never done before. I smiled at the woman and said, "I'm sorry, not right now. It's just not a good time. Hopefully we'll get a chance to take a photo and talk in the future."

My reply shocked her. It shocked me too. I wouldn't be surprised if she walked away thinking that I'm a total self-centered bitch. Maybe she even shared the experience with others. I felt awful for rejecting her, but everything inside me was telling me to prioritize my son.

Sometimes we have to disappoint people in order to not disappoint ourselves.

I trusted myself that day.

Luka has his own path. I deluded myself into thinking that my version of him is what's best for him because my version felt safe to me. But what's really best for him is encouraging him to trust himself. I don't want him to give power to others to dictate who he is or what his story should look like.

And *others* includes me.

"Help me understand what it's like to be you," I'll ask my kids now every once in a while. And then I listen.

I'm realizing more and more how so many of the mistakes

I made throughout parenting came from speeding ahead following someone else's directions, trusting that the "ideal" framework maps my best path.

In the past, whenever Luka was trying to make a decision or pondering something about life, my natural urge was to give him my best advice. I wanted him to push ahead, using the road map I had internalized as his directions. Following everyone else's advice was what I did when faced with decisions. These days I try to slow down. Instead of offering my take, I ask Luka, "What do *you* believe? What do *you* think is the next right step? Which decision would make *you* the most proud?" When I manage to do this, I'm able to see how much healthier and more empowering listening feels than all the energy I and many of my generation have spent pining after our parents' approval. I don't want Luka, or his siblings, to live for my approval. And on those extra-tough days when his insecurities feel amplified, I need him to know that depression and anxiety don't diminish his wisdom and insight, and that he is still capable of making smart decisions that he can feel proud of.

During our journey together through these tough years, I would often feel my anger at Luka flare up. He'd snap at me, ignore me, act entitled or ungrateful in the moment, and suddenly I'd find myself enraged. The emotional intensity felt physically unhealthy. My chest would tighten, my heart would race. Taking a slow, deep breath felt almost impossible. And then I would put pressure on myself in that moment to relax, but trying to find the inner calm felt like trying to find Waldo, and it only increased my stress. The grip of this overpowering sensation peeled away layers of rational thinking, leaving me feeling unsteady and completely vulnerable. Once the adrenaline would finally subside, deep sadness would take over, as if I had been defeated by the worst parts of me.

While learning to support Luka through his struggles, I had to make an intentional choice to delve deeper into my own. The inability to change another person or a situation leaves us with two options: keep trying and die trying, or shift our focus. Instead of fixing my gaze on what is beyond my control, what I wished I could change, I challenged myself to look more closely at the things within me that need my healing attention—and that I could actually impact. I started digging into the root of my anger at Luka, trying to understand why it feels so overwhelming to manage at times. After doing what I do best—overthinking—I came to an important realization: The instances of intense rage are not so much about being angry at Luka or about the surface-level circumstances of the moment. The person I'm actually angry at is myself. At first, I fought against this notion. How did it even make sense, especially during the times when Luka's conduct so obviously justified my reaction? But ultimately there was no denying that my anger was a symptom of my underlying worry that I am lacking, that I am not enough. My anger was screaming: What does Luka's behavior or the situation we find ourselves in say about me?

My anger spans multiple layers. I am angry that I don't know how to fix things, that no matter how hard I try, I can't always come up with an effective way to help my child. Some of the layers are about regrets over the mistakes I've made, the scenarios I thought I was navigating well, only to later recognize my complete mishandling. And then there's the layer of scrutiny—wondering what I could have done differently when Luka was young that could've perhaps kept us from reaching this crisis. I'm fully aware and accepting of the fact that it is impossible for any parent to be perfect, but still, am I a good enough mother, teacher, example, support system? Have I set my child up for a healthy, happy, productive life? Have I failed my child?

In all honesty, the self-criticism wasn't just about Luka. Over the years, whenever any of my children stepped into the realm of my insecurities, my anger at myself (masked as anger at them and rationalized as typical parental stress) would make an appearance. I can add this to the long list of insights I wish I had grasped much earlier.

I'd worked hard over the years to wrestle with anger, and

even before I understood just how profoundly my anger was tied to my insecurities, I had made great strides in keeping my anger off my kids. I worked hard not to raise my voice. I worked hard to take space when I needed it. But the rage was still there, roaring inside me. Outwardly, I came across as a parent who was calmer and more patient than she had been in her younger years, but on the inside, I was still spiraling.

Even the mere awareness, this fresh understanding about my anger, has helped me pause when I feel my chest begin to tighten. I try to give myself a gentle reminder to resist the tendency to become too enmeshed. Not everyone and everything around me are a mirror of my worth or identity. Including my children.

Learning to separate the self-judgment from my kids' struggles, mistakes, meltdowns, setbacks, and poor choices allows me to genuinely listen and empathize, instead of immediately rushing to fix, rescue, or reprimand. It's almost impossible for me to show unconditional love and offer unwavering encouragement to someone when I'm operating from a place of self-rage. Every encounter I have with someone is influenced by the aspects of myself that still need healing. The relationship I have with myself affects all other relationships I am a part of.

In every interaction with my child, I can choose to either control or connect. But I can't do both, because reaching for control always pulls me out of the range of connection. I never had the power to save Luka. I didn't have the power to force him to make healthy choices. *But a good mother would know how. Her child would respect her enough to listen to her, to obey her.* Even now I can hear those old voices whispering to me. But it's a lie.

These days, I try to find a moment to check in with Luka and ask, "How can I support you today?" I find that question soothing. It feels like love that's free of control or expectation. A love that says, *I want you to trust yourself.*

A few weeks before Luka's peers will graduate from high school, I run into an old acquaintance in the parking lot of Trader Joe's. I haven't seen this woman in years, but her son and Luka had some classes together at Luka's old school and would hang out occasionally. As we start chatting, she says, "Can you believe our boys are already graduating this year? Where did the time go?"

I pause for a moment and then say the only thing I can think of that's true. "They grow up fast."

She continues, "Are you guys having a graduation party? We're back and forth, trying to decide whether to keep it small with just family or throw a big party."

Suddenly I feel myself falling off the steady path I've found and back into that old pit of lava. I feel the uncomfortable pressure that comes from living outside the ideal framework the world has set for us. I consider keeping my answers vague and saying something like, "Oh, we've been so busy, we haven't figured out our plans yet!"

But instead, heart racing, I decide to meet the moment with ease and truth. "Luka actually is not graduating," I declare.

"Oh." The woman looks surprised, and as if she's a little embarrassed. Maybe for her, maybe for me, maybe for both of us. With a sadness in her voice, she adds, "I'm so sorry."

I smile, my heart still racing. "No, no. It's good. He's been working on his mental health and is making so much progress. I'm really proud of him. And I know he's proud of himself too."

Weathering her response takes something that felt big and makes it uncomplicated, manageable. Being straightforward about our situation helps me realize that I'm very much okay with our truth. It finally feels as though clarity and vulnerability are no longer a source of unease, but instead are a comforting reassurance that I'm finally in a place where I am accepting of and embracing our story.

Five months later, Luka completes his final coursework and earns his high school diploma. It will be mailed to him without any special commemoration. But I don't want him to miss out on celebrating this achievement. He deserves just as much fanfare as any other kid, so I plan a surprise graduation ceremony for him. Friends are invited, the living room is decorated, the chairs are lined up in rows for the "audience." I create ceremony programs. Because he's the only one graduating that specific day, I decide this automatically makes him the valedictorian, a detail I make sure to mention in the program.

The evening of the surprise ceremony, our family takes Luka out for dinner. When we arrive home, the house is filled with guests, and "Pomp and Circumstance," the graduation march, is playing. Luka looks genuinely moved. I take the cap and gown I have ordered online, and help him get dressed. Friends and family take turns walking up to the fake podium I made by stacking two tree stumps on top of each other, and they give heartfelt speeches. Luka is sitting in the front row, taking in all the admiration. A friend of mine shares a story about how much it meant to her family when they overheard Luka encouraging her brother-in-law, who was struggling too. His loved ones share how proud they are of him, how they watched him struggle and not give up, how honored they are to be a part of this big day.

Luka graduating doesn't actually come five months late. It comes right on time. His time.

Lie #10

You Can't Eat
a Meatball
Sandwich Cold

During a vacation to visit my parents in Croatia, Ari and I spend the night in my childhood bedroom. Each time I'm in this room, I'm swept back in time, surrounded by a cascade of memories that have stayed vivid through the years. This was home. This will always feel like home. It's a beautifully tender experience to be able to intertwine my little boy's childhood with mine.

Upon entering the room, Ari immediately notices the jagged holes in the old wooden window blinds. Last time we were here, he was too young to really pay attention to them. Now I tell him the story of how during the war in Croatia, when I was twelve years old, a grenade hit somewhere near our house and shrapnel from the grenade flew through my window and destroyed a part of my room. Thankfully I was not in my bedroom when this took place; otherwise I'm not sure I'd be here today. The window has been fixed since, but the blinds remain damaged. Ari's curiosity fills the evening with questions, and we stay up late, talking.

Early the next morning, I wake up and see him sitting up in the bed, his eyes fixated on the damaged blinds. He stares at them quietly for a few minutes, then says, "Mommy, but it looks beautiful when the light comes through."

I'm standing at the stove, sautéing onions for the chicken marsala I'm preparing for dinner. Luka is walking straight toward me. As he approaches me, I can feel my body stiffen. He was in a bad mood earlier, so I'm filled with a nauseating dread. I have gotten used to him taking his pain out on me. But as Luka gets closer, he wraps his arms around me gently, gives me a hug, makes a joke, and then goes on with his day.

My posture softens. My shoulders relax. I exhale.

I notice I have a missed call and a voicemail from Luka's therapist. Why would he call? He never calls me anymore. Luka sets his own appointments now. My heart immediately sinks, anticipating the therapist breaking confidentiality with Luka in order to inform me of the next scary situation we will need to handle. I nervously listen to the voicemail. His call is about updating our insurance information. No bad news.

My posture softens. My shoulders relax. I exhale.

I wake up in the middle of the night and head downstairs to get a glass of water. Out of habit, I look down the hall. I notice that Luka's bedroom door is wide open. My back tenses. I walk over and see that his bed is empty. He's not in his room. I take the stairs two at a time as I run down to see if Luka is in the kitchen or asleep on the couch. I can't find him anywhere. I am immediately drenched in fear. I run back upstairs and wake up Philip. Half asleep, he answers, "He's sleeping over at Brandon's. Remember? He told us that."

My posture softens. My shoulders relax. I exhale.

Sometimes I seem to be doing well. I'm fine. Then out of the blue, I'm not okay.

I'm struggling.

I'm surprisingly great.

I'm not doing so well.

And then I'm good again.

Scratch that. I'm feeling terrible.

I've hit a breaking point.

I'm feeling nothing.

I'm feeling everything.

I'm sobbing.

I'm better.

I'm worse.

I'm so-so.

I'm not well at all.

When I go through my mental checklist, everyone and everything in my life are somewhat okay right now, so I've been trying to figure out why I'm not. And I'm realizing that while I was busy the past few years working on supporting Luka the best I knew how, while also trying to be there for my other kids, and nurturing my marriage and friendships, and navigating a career, and, and, and . . . I ran out of time to deal with myself. I was in support groups with Luka and in therapy with him, but there was so much to process that I never got to the stuff beneath the stuff. It's kind of like when you clean your home just enough so you can function in it, but under the facade of semi-order, there's still so much to go through and organize and clean up, and it feels like you'll never get to it all because just the little daily cleanups take so much time that there's never enough time or energy for the deep cleaning and organizing.

And then I realize that I've started judging my own emotions and feeling like it's weird to even voice how hard it all is when my child is the one who has been really suffering. I don't want to make it all about me. And yet by not tending to my own pain and struggles, I've ended up in this funk that feels poised to taint everything around me.

I make an appointment with a therapist a friend recommends to me. His name is Paul and he offers virtual sessions, which is a blessing when life feels like a lot and all I want is to stay in soft clothes and slippers for the rest of my forever. As I log on to our first video chat, I see Paul's window pop up on-screen. His smile is friendly and warm. "Hi, there!" he says.

I don't want to overwhelm him, so at first I decide to give him a few quick, simple thoughts on why I think I need therapy. Unsurprisingly, I end up completely unloading instead, cramming in as many details as possible within our fifty-minute session.

"I think I might have PTSD. I'm definitely parenting out of fear, which I know is sucky parenting, and that fear pushes me into this stupid need to control everything even though I'm fully aware that I have zero control over most things and all people—a rather unfortunate truth, by the way—and then that realization gives me severe anxiety. Or did the anxiety come first, causing the need to control? Chicken or the egg? Anyway . . . I have thought about and talked about and sat with and felt and cried all my feelings. I've processed my feelings so much that they're overprocessed—they are now Cheetos. I understand my past trauma, and yet knowing the what and why and how isn't helping me right now. And I never know whether I am a dramatic person or the situations in my life actually are dramatic, so my 'dramatic' responses to them are completely appropriate. And often my body feels like it's prepped and ready for the next trauma, like I've packed my disaster supply kit and I'm just waiting for the next emotional hurricane to hit. And weirdly, at the same time, I feel this sense of confidence. I don't care what anyone thinks of me or my son or our family. I know that whatever comes next, I will handle it. I think I'm just really tired. I'm really, really tired. And also sad? Yeah. Sad. Sometimes it feels as if I'm grieving the person I was before all this happened, before my days became consumed with fear that I will lose my child."

There's an absurdity to how I'm feeling, but it's very real. It's like I'm drowning, struggling to catch my breath, with an unceasing weight pressing down on my chest.

As I share more of my story, Paul listens intently, his eyes always reflecting empathy. His questions and responses feel like he's slowly walking me across a bridge, guiding me away from my jumbled mess and into a space of clarity and understanding.

My mind is hypervigilant when it comes to any potential warning signs with Luka. I can't help but notice every little detail and then weave them into my narrative of fear. It's like the time I was contemplating purchasing a new car. After settling on a specific make and model, I suddenly started noticing that car on the road every day, often multiple times a day. Obviously there wasn't a sudden surge of people in my town purchasing the vehicle I had my eye on. Those cars had already been there for a long time. But now the image of this car was etched so deeply in my mind that it occupied a significant portion of my thoughts, leading me to constantly notice it.

Once Luka started struggling, I transformed into a very astute observer of his well-being. I became so attuned to every facet of his life—his moods, actions, circumstances, everything he was doing, often hour to hour.

The brain tends to recruit the things that support our point of view. My point of view for years has been: *Luka is in danger. I should be worried about Luka.* So now, even on days that are good, my brain instructs me to look for evidence that will prove my fear is justified. I have become alert to even the slightest potential indications that Luka is severely struggling, even if they're completely irrational. This is unfair to him and cruel to me.

I'm at a sandwich shop one afternoon, and I decide to call Luka to see if he'd like me to pick up a sandwich for him. He tells me he'd love a meatball sandwich. There's something really nice about just being able to call Luka without any sense of dread, ask him a simple question, and receive a simple answer.

I arrive home with the meatball sandwich and inform him that it's in the kitchen. He yells from his bedroom that he'll come down soon. This might sound like a normal exchange, but the word *soon* makes me a little nervous. Soon is not a designated unit of time. And this is a meatball sandwich. It's not a cold sandwich. It's meant to be eaten warm. I'm worried about the meatballs cooling down. I'm worried about the red sauce soaking the bread, and the bread getting all soggy and gross. I'm worried about a lot of stuff. But I decide to be patient and just let it go. He'll come down. So I'm patient and I give him approximately seventeen seconds. Then I call out again, "Hey, come eat your sandwich while it's still warm." Luka screams down, "All right, thanks, Mom."

That response is very upsetting to me. I don't know whether he means "Thanks, I'm coming right now," or "Thanks, I'll get to it sooooon." I start pondering if I should try to rescue the sandwich. Maybe I could extract the meatballs and scrape the sauce off the bread to keep it from getting soggy. Then he could reheat the meatballs separately. If need be, he could put the meatballs on different, non-soggy bread. Maybe there's a way to save the sandwich and not lose all respect for my son. But I take a deep breath and decide to wait. I wait another ninety seconds, which is a lifetime in meatball sandwich years. And I'm starting to wonder, *What kind of an emotionally stable person would settle for a cold, soggy meatball sandwich?* If he settles for a cold, soggy meatball sandwich, what else will he settle for in life? I don't want my son to give up on his dreams like he's obviously given up on this sandwich.

At this point I decide that I need to bring in backup. I go to Philip and I tell him about the awful situation we find ourselves in as a family, about the sandwich that is decomposing and how you can't undo a sog. I ask him to please have a chat with Luka, transmit this urgency to him, and make him come downstairs. Philip gives me a hug, looks at me, and says, "No. I'm not gonna do that. You shouldn't either. Let it go." And that's when I decide to file for divorce. Not really. But as far as I was concerned, the move would have been justified.

Philip is a really good, caring man, but it has always bothered me that whenever we've gone through hard times as a family, he hasn't seemed to be as affected by the stress as I am. At times, I've wondered whether he even cares as much as I do. Sure, he deals with problems head-on and takes care of things that need to be taken care of, but so often when everything feels chaotic, I find him looking all relaxed, calm, as if our world isn't completely falling apart.

Recently I had an epiphany. In those moments, I'm not actually mad at Philip. I'm jealous. It's not that the hard parts of our life don't affect him. It's just that he doesn't allow them to destroy him. Instead of judging him, I could be learning from him.

A few days later I'm telling Paul about the meatball sandwich and how all I wanted was for Luka to just come downstairs immediately and eat. Paul nods in his sage way, then says,

"All you wanted, Kristina, was for him to be normal. Whatever feels normal and safe to you."

Whoa.

I sit there speechless, lost in contemplation. My eyes are getting misty. It dawns on me that all the time I spent dramatically plotting out my son's tragic future, a spiral that started because of a meatball sandwich—maybe (and by maybe, I mean definitely) my stress had nothing to do with the actual sandwich. My stress was about the story I created around the sandwich, not the sandwich itself. By now, I am aware that I don't have control over Luka's mental health struggles. I don't have control of the roller coaster our family has been on for the past four years. I don't have control over his future. But I figured, Hey, maybe I at least have control over a meatball sandwich. When Luka didn't behave in whatever way I decided was normal in that second, my anxiety started provoking me: *He doesn't want to eat right now because he's really depressed. He's struggling. You should be worried about him.* And I needed my son to show me that he was okay by fitting into my "this is how you behave when you're healthy" box.

Anxiety is a prolific storyteller.

I turn my feelings into beliefs, my beliefs into facts, and facts into actions. I feel anxious, therefore I believe there's a legitimate reason to be anxious, which means something is definitely wrong, so I'd better assert control in any way I can in order to fix it. Or more truthfully, to alleviate the agonizing, chronic, all-consuming fear that's suffocating me.

When I operate from a place of fear, I'm giving the world the absolute worst version of myself: a self that's far from clearheaded, a self who is only willing to settle for what I've imagined as the best outcome, a self that can't seem to free herself from the role of a domineering puppeteer.

The more I focus on the bad, the blurrier the good becomes. I need to pay more attention to the evidence of all that is good. Luka continues to prioritize his mental health. He has healthy hobbies he's committed to. He communicates openly with us. He no longer has episodes of uncontrolled rage. He isn't isolating. He isn't misusing substances. He isn't numbing his feelings. He fulfills his work commitments. He's paying for his car. He spends time with friends and loved ones.

The hard stuff in life is much easier when I decide to just focus on the thing, instead of creating stories around the thing.

On top of the PTSD the past few years caused, I am also trying to adjust to the normal struggles of letting go of a child who is now an adult. My seemingly relentless fear still shows up to push me toward micromanaging everything. Luka and I have worked so hard on our relationship, and Paul points out that if I can't pull back, Luka is likely to pull away. When I see Luka sleeping more than I feel he should, instead of panicking that it's a sign of severe depression or potential suicidality and then telling him he needs to get up, I have to refrain and back off. When I'm worried Luka might be late to his psychiatry appointment, which I am now no longer a part of, I need to zip it. When I feel like he should be eating healthier, I need to keep that to myself unless he seeks my guidance. If I wouldn't want my parent now commenting on every decision I make, I should give him the same respect. This adjustment is undeniably challenging. Not only did I take care of so many of his needs while he was growing up, but the past few years I was exhausting myself, trying to do everything I could to keep him alive. And now I'm expected to step back. Adapting to parenting an adult child often feels like major culture shock.

During a session with Paul, we are discussing my past, and how so many events in my life, from a young age, caused me to believe that I have to do and fix in order to survive. Now I'm constantly in fight-or-flight mode. So much of my value has been predicated on how much I can control the outcome of any given situation, and this was especially true while trying to help Luka the past few years. Even though I knew I couldn't control much, holding on to control has been a way of staving off the fear that tells me I'm not doing enough. Paul says, "Kristina, you've had to be in charge every time. But see, now that has to change. Luka is moving to his own adulthood. That's going to look like what it's going to look like. You will love him, you will support him. Those are the places where you show up for him every single time and I have no doubt in my mind that he knows that. But you cannot lead him at every step. When you hit a point where you're starting to buzz inside, and you're feeling really stressed out, that is your cue right there that you are too close and you gotta pull back. Keep working on taking that step of interrupting the cycle, stopping the intrusive thoughts. And if you can do that, you will start to notice a shift. It's hard work. It's a lot of focus in practice. But you will get through it. You will. You've gotten through rough stuff before."

I am working on retraining my brain, which is harder than I anticipated when I first realized I was in need of substantial cognitive adjustments. So, when the piercing sirens and the flashing warning lights activate in my head, I make a conscious effort to pull the mental emergency brake and reassess: This is what is actually happening today. These are the facts. No need to start creating scenarios around them. Ashley's words echo in my mind: "This move is hard and you might need to take a pause. That's okay. Take what you need and don't make a whole story about it."

Paul is teaching me the art of surrender. Or as I call it, the art of pretending I'm an entirely different person with an entirely different brain.

What does it even mean to surrender? To me, surrender has always sounded like complacency.

But maybe surrendering doesn't mean giving up. Maybe it means opening up. Maybe it means taking a breath and instead of doing, just being. Maybe it means finding peace even while sitting in uncertainty.

Instead of operating from a place of fear, what would it look like if I chose to treat Luka as if he's the healthiest version of himself? Maybe approaching him in that manner would help him start to see himself that way too. What if I also started asking myself, when confronted with fear or anxiety: How would the healthiest version of me handle this situation? Instead of what can I *do* for Luka, who can I *be* for him?

I cannot control what happens next in Luka's story. His journey, like everyone else's, is unpredictable and his own. The least brave choice I could make is to allow the worry I feel about the stuff I can't control to distract me from the good I can contribute.

One evening, as Matea is telling me about the latest drama that happened at her restaurant job, I come up with an analogy. "Matea, I noticed that you tend to pick up everything like it's a brick. Life will hand you a lot of actual bricks that you have no control over, so if you choose to pick up everything else as a brick also, every day will feel really heavy. Some things can be feathers. So always just ask yourself, 'Does this have to be a brick, or can it be a feather?' If it's a feather, acknowledge it and then watch it drift away."

She doesn't say much and I assume she's silently dismissing my analogy. But as I'm talking with her, I start to realize that I need this visual as much as I think she does. Probably more. I don't have to assign brick weight to every little worry or slipup or annoyance that I encounter with Luka. Some things can be feathers.

The following evening, Matea comes home from work and I ask her how it went.

"Good!" she replies.

"Good? You never say work was good. What happened?"

"Feathers!" She smiles at me and runs off to her room.

In a session with Paul I tell him that I'm writing this book.

"I don't know if I made the right decision. Every time I sit to write, my body is fighting it, as if it's guarding itself somehow. My brain freezes, not like a typical writer's block, but more like an aversion to returning to a dark cave when I finally feel like we're out. The last few years have been filled with so much fear and pain. Why would I willingly revisit that now, especially so soon? This book, our story, it all feels so heavy."

Paul is silent for a moment, then says, "What you're feeling is the shadow of trauma. But try to release yourself from the dark. This book you're writing about you and Luka is a love story. You are writing a love story."

The world around me slows down, and the words he's chosen hit me like the notes of a familiar song I forgot I knew yet remember every word to. I smile. A tear glides down my cheek, and I can feel goose bumps on my skin. Paul's simple yet profound words beautifully capture the chapters of the past few years, even—or perhaps especially—the most painful ones. This is a love story.

From Luka

I've always felt a little different. But life didn't seem like a struggle until I was around twelve years old. Suddenly, everything that was fun seemed less fun. Nothing was good enough. Something was always missing. Even the temperature felt colder somehow. When I look back now, I remember having all kinds of intense emotions that I couldn't fully understand or define, so I would suppress them just to get through a school day or social gathering. I'd put on a mask to hide how miserable I felt, and I'd wear it for as long as I had to. Then the instant I took that mask off, I'd explode.

Being diagnosed with depression (and later anxiety and ADHD) in some ways felt like a relief because I finally had an explanation for what I was experiencing, but the diagnosis also felt like yet another big unknown I had to deal with when I already didn't want to deal with anything.

For me, depression wasn't just something I felt. It was physical too. I was completely exhausted. My heart felt ten pounds heavier. My lungs felt clogged, like I couldn't breathe. Sometimes I had an intense headache. And everything, every single thing, felt harder to do. Even something as simple as brushing my teeth or going to the bathroom. Depression could at times overpower all my basic needs. And the less I took care of myself, the less I wanted to be around people. The less I was around people, the less motivated I was to care for myself.

Anxiety felt like everyone was paying attention to me, analyzing my every move. I worried that if I made a mistake, something terrible would happen and it would be all my fault. Even taking medication for anxiety made me anxious because I worried I'd forget to take it. Anxiety basically made me feel stupid. And that feeling only added to the depression.

I felt stuck. Stuck in a cloud where I couldn't even remember good times. And I felt trapped, like everything was working at keeping me from making any progress.

My suicidal thoughts would start off with immense depression. I'd stop caring. Life was too much for me. Maybe I'd laugh at a joke or something, but I was beginning to feel like it had been years since I felt real joy. I'd replay all the moments I did something wrong or the people I've hurt. I felt like a piece of shit. I'd feel anger that I'm alive. And then I'd start asking myself: *Why don't you kill yourself?*

Sometimes it felt like I just had to stay alive for everyone else to be okay, so I wouldn't hurt them. At other times, I felt like I was a massive problem, like I would do people in my life a favor if I was gone.

I was one of those kids who completely shut out the adults in my life. *Oh, you're here to support me? I don't want anything to do with you. No one will ever understand me, and I want to get through this by myself.*

And I didn't open up to kids my age about how I was feeling because I didn't want to give them ammunition to bully me. So, I didn't share with anyone. I didn't ask for help.

Every day felt long and the same and heavy, and the only thoughts that played on repeat in my mind were of how much I hated myself.

I started dealing with my pain in unproductive ways. I slept all day. And even when I couldn't sleep, I would just lie in bed, staring at the ceiling. I would scream awful things at my parents. I took out my anger on the people I love the most because I knew they wouldn't leave me.

The first time I tried alcohol, I had a good day. I hadn't had a good day in years. The effects of alcohol felt nice and I felt free.

So I started coping with my depression by numbing out with drugs and alcohol. I couldn't be happy without being drunk or high. I would tell my friends, "I haven't taken my meds yet," referring to drugs. The weed I was getting from other kids was usually laced with something that would really mess me up. That routine got real nasty, real quick. Chasing drugs helped me justify stealing in order to self-medicate. It helped me justify screaming at my family. It helped me justify making a lot of incredibly selfish and hurtful choices. Yelling and fighting and doing drugs felt good in those moments, but ultimately all they did was leave me feeling even more depressed.

I needed somebody to blame for how I was feeling. Blaming someone else was much easier than looking closely at myself. From my perspective at the time, the pain I felt was all my mom's fault. She was the one who stole my drugs, so she was the reason I ended up in the hospital. I blamed any adult figure in my life who had any rules or expectations of me. In my mind, my anger at everyone else was justified, and I didn't see my part in it at all. I wasn't even willing to consider someone else's point of view or experience.

I can't remember many specific moments from that time. My memories are made up of scattered bits and pieces, all foggy. I'm sure the drugs I was on contributed to my lack of memory. But depression was a big factor too. Because it consumed me, I wasn't really paying attention to much else. And to be honest, I don't even want to try to remember that time.

It was miserable and lonely and I have no desire to revisit the details.

What I know is that my life was starting to fall apart. But it took a while to admit this to myself. I knew that my grades were plummeting, that my relationship with my family was getting worse and worse, and that I had a serious problem with how I was handling it all. Seeing everything in my life deteriorating made me realize I needed to make some changes. I needed help.

Often, just working on mental health feels like it takes too much energy, and when you're already exhausted, it's easy to give up on putting in any effort. There's no quick fix and that can get very frustrating. We've learned to want things quickly. Especially now, with technology, the internet . . . everything is immediate. We expect things to be instantly good if we just try once. But it takes a lifetime commitment to stay healthy. And for me, it helped having people who were willing to walk the long road with me.

For a while, my mom and I would find ourselves stuck in a place that wasn't helpful to either of us. When I got loud and annoyed, my mom would match my energy. I understood even then that it's really hard not to get loud when someone is screaming at you, but this kind of confrontation just led to both of us escalating and making the situation more extreme than it had to be. Over time, my mom got good at not meeting my anger with anger. I knew I had to work on staying calm too. I'm not trying to excuse my behavior toward her, but it does help when the parent can stay calm in those situations. (Of course, when I'm a dad someday, I'm sure I'll be perfectly Zen no matter what my kids do.)

When my parents complimented me, it would just remind me of all the things I was lacking. If someone told me that I'm smart, I would immediately think of every time I did something wrong or stupid. Often, when my mom would ask what she could do to help, I'd brush her off with "Nothing." Or she'd ask how I'm doing, and I'd say "Fine" in a way that shut down any more conversation. I was trying to get through each interaction as quickly as possible by giving the shortest answers. I just wanted the conversation to end. That's the attitude I had when I was at my lowest. My mom started ending every one of those conversations with a reminder that if I ever need anything, I could come to her and talk to her. By repeatedly saying that to me, she instilled those reminders in my brain. And eventually, when I felt like I really needed to talk to someone, her words were so ingrained in me that I did come to her and I opened up.

Looking back now, I can see how important it was that my mom didn't give up on saying supportive things to me. Even when I acted like I didn't care or I ignored her, I still heard her. A lot of the times it's the person struggling who has to initiate reaching out. They have to want the help. But they won't reach out unless you set that space where they feel safe and know that they can come to you at any time.

What has helped me a lot is knowing that my home is a place where I can talk about anything and everything. Nothing is taboo. No topic is shut down. I'm sure certain conversations are uncomfortable, and it must be really hard for parents not to feel consumed by worry, but when parents come from a place of just worrying, kids don't feel safe. It took a long time to realize that my parents genuinely cared and were trying. They wanted the best for me, even if they didn't always know how to get there. When I was in pain, it was easy to use any mistakes they made against them. But now I don't think about the times my parents messed up. I think about the ways my parents supported me. I had to stop seeing them as my enemies and start seeing them as part of my team. When we're struggling, what stands out to us kids is how different we are from everyone else. We isolate ourselves. It was always helpful when my parents found ways to relate to my feelings and emotions. *I don't understand the exact way you're feeling, the extent of it, but I've felt similar things . . .*

As well as you think you know your kid, you don't really know what they're feeling and thinking—so listen. Don't assume you know what's going on and what needs to be done. Take a step back, don't judge, and be okay with not knowing but wanting to learn.

I've been asked by multiple doctors and therapists what I think contributed to my depression and anxiety. Whether there's a deeper cause or reason, I don't know, but what matters now is that I continue doing the things that I know will help. I don't want the *why* about my depression to distract me from the *what*: What can I do right now that might help me deal with my mental health struggles?

It's important for me to listen to how my body is feeling. If I'm feeling down, feeling heavy, getting more easily frustrated, not wanting to do anything . . . those are signs I need to pay attention to. Now when I feel myself falling back to old unhealthy patterns, I stop and take a second. Instead of exploding and screaming, I take a breath, and then find the energy to do something more productive with my discomfort. I do ten push-ups or go punch a punching bag, go play a game of chess, or do whatever hobby I'm into at the time. Hobbies are such an important tool in mental health. They give me something that feels fulfilling, they help me focus on doing something creative or positive. They can distract me from dwelling on the negative thoughts, they can get me involved in a community. Doing nothing only leaves me feeling more depressed. Replacing something that's damaging with something that actually helps me grow is valuable. I try to find ways to make myself proud.

I also think it's important to surround myself with people who are willing to be honest about and work on their mental health. Support groups were a big step for me toward health. Those groups gave me a place to communicate openly without being nervous that I wouldn't be accepted. When I'm anxious, I'm constantly worrying. It might only be three things I'm worrying about, but I keep repeating them in my head so many times that three things start feeling like a hundred things. Once I share my thoughts with someone, once I say them out loud, they feel lighter. What's alone in my head always feels heavier.

The phrases I used to tell myself—*I'm not enough; something bad will happen; I don't look good; I'm gonna get fired from my job*—still come up in my mind, but now I try to immediately take notice and challenge my thoughts. It's important to catch myself before I get deeper into negativity. Instead of staying in the anxiety, I tell myself: *You've taken this too far. You might have these thoughts, but they are not true.* And then I try to go do something productive.

I'm far from perfect at dealing with my mental health. Even after all the help and tools I've received, I can get very lazy. But I know that I can't just sit on my butt, do nothing, and expect things to get better. I've tried that many times. I still like to test it out every once in a while. Shockingly, the result is always the same.

For a while, I was embarrassed that I have anxiety and depression. It was hard for me to say out loud to certain people that I struggle. And I definitely didn't want people knowing I went to a psychiatric hospital. What really helped me was attending support groups. Hearing about someone else's day, their stories and experiences, and seeing the way they face their hardships helped me realize I'm not abnormal. It wasn't a light-bulb moment; it was a slow process, but now I'm very open. A lot of times when I meet someone, within the first ten minutes of talking to them, I will confidently mention that I have mental health struggles. I don't carry shame. We should only feel shame or embarrassment for something bad we purposely did, and I have felt that for the horrible things I did and all the ways I hurt my loved ones. I've owned my mistakes and asked for forgiveness. But why should I feel shame for my diagnosis? I didn't choose to have mental illness. I didn't choose to feel the way I feel. That's out of my control. I don't have to be perfect. I don't have to put on a fake face. I don't have to pretend everything is fine. I look at all that I've been through as a part of my story. It's a part of who I am and there's no need to hide who I am. And if somebody chooses to judge me, that's on them. Not my problem and I won't waste time on it.

I still struggle. There are days when everything looks good on paper: I'm not using negative coping skills. I have friends. I have a supportive girlfriend. I'm doing hobbies. And yet even on those seemingly good days, I'm not always doing well. Mental health can often feel like a tug of war—sometimes I'm winning, sometimes I'm losing. I will never achieve perfect mental health, but there are so many reasons I want to be here today: to discover my passions, to be in love, to have good friends, to continue to be close with my family . . . I'm looking forward to my future. I'm looking forward to getting married one day, having kids, traveling the world, and even just little things like having a good laugh.

Life gets better, but we have to put in the work. We have to choose to keep putting in the work, sometimes without seeing any benefits at first. But eventually they come. The work will pay off. And it will be worth it.

I'm glad I'm still here.

Acknowledgments

I feel a sense of apprehension letting this book slip out of my hands and into the world. As a mother, my hope is that Luka's courage in allowing me to share his darkest days will be met with kindness and without judgment. While this book is deeply personal, it would not exist without the collaborative effort of others.

Luka: Throughout writing these chapters, every time I asked you whether I have your permission to share a very private, vulnerable moment from your life, your response was always "Write it." Thank you for guiding me through your stories, sharing your perspective and insights to ensure authenticity to your lived experiences. I have so much respect for your openness and your desire to help others feel less alone. Volim te do neba visoko.

ACKNOWLEDGMENTS

Philip: I couldn't have written this book without you, emotionally or logistically. You never once complained when you had to carry the bigger load in our family and home in order for me to finish these pages. You sat with me for hours as I navigated the storm of emotions brought on by writing this book. And you were so gracious to allow me to share a part of our story so publicly. I love you more than bread.

Laura (my editor at Penguin Random House): Nothing I've ever done careerwise has felt as nerve-racking as writing this book. You were so patient with the constant changes I was making, continually guiding me and helping me find the right words when I felt stuck. I especially, *especially* want to thank you for being so kind to Luka and respectful of his story.

Anna (my literary agent at Neon): For knowing this part of my (and Luka's) life should be a book, and then making it happen. And also, for the multiple, all-caps, elated texts you sent me after reading the manuscript for the first time. They gave me the courage to release my tight grip on this book.

Matea, Ari, Judy, Lou: All of you, in your own ways, helped me get to the finish line. Whether it was Judy and Lou babysitting, Matea keeping Ari busy so I could focus, or both of the kids being extra patient with me when I had deadlines that required my full attention . . . I love you all so much.

Jo, Cat, Amy, Zach: The unwavering support you've given me through all the years I've known you is the greatest gift I never realized how much I needed. I'm so grateful for all of you and your wisdom.

Paul: I would like to thank myself (from you) for my dramatic life that ensures you're never bored during our therapy sessions. You're welcome. (And also, you're damn good at your job.)

Jacy Patt: You are an angel. Thank you for always showing up for my family. Thank you for empowering hundreds of kids to remove their masks, to be fully seen and fully loved.

Neela: How fortunate am I to have your friendship, wisdom, and medical expertise in my life. Thank you for answering my every call or text, despite your already very full life.

Rich: Thank you for believing for me things I can't yet even imagine, and guiding me toward them.

All the kids and families I met in support groups: I found comfort and healing in your bravery and transparency. All my love to you.

My viewers and readers: Your support and kindness throughout the years have given me so many wonderful, scary, and life-changing opportunities. I appreciate you.

Anyone I left out who feels they should be mentioned: Thank you, and I apologize for my lack of brain cells. #motherhood